WIT

&

WISDOM

OF MISSOURI'S COUNTRY EDITORS

Bill Robinson

Wm H. Taft

whitpenny@aol.com

WIT
&
WISDOM

OF MISSOURI'S COUNTRY EDITORS

Compiled by
William H. Taft

with a foreword by
Bill Tammeus, of the *Kansas City Star*

Illustrations by Peggy Guest

Pebble Publishing
Columbia, Missouri

Project support by Pebble Publishing staff:
Brett Dufur, Daisy Dufur, Pippa Letsky and Heather Starek

ISBN 0-9646625-3-1 14.95
Copyright © 1996 by William Taft
All other rights © 1996 by Pebble Publishing

Pebble Publishing, P.O. Box 431, Columbia, MO 65205-0431
Phone: (573) 698-3903 Fax: (573) 698-3108
E-Mail: pebble@global-image.com

Printed by Ovid Bell Press, Fulton, Missouri, USA

Dedicated to

Those Pioneer Missouri Editors

Who had the courage to say what they thought

And the talent to make their comments amusing

As well as the ability to stir their readers to action,

And to my wife, Myrtle,

Who listened to me as I recited

So many of these remarks so often

To anyone who would listen.

Our republic and its press will rise or fall together. An able, disinterested, public spirited press, with trained intelligence to know the right and courage to do it, can preserve that public virtue without which popular government is a sham and a mockery. A cynical, mercenary, demagogic press will produce in time a people as base as itself. The power to mould the future of the republic will be in the hands of the journalists of future generations.

— Joseph Pulitzer, 1904
North American Review

Acknowledgments

S pecial thanks to the State Historical Society of Missouri in Columbia, where there are more than 35,000,000 pages of Missouri newspapers on microfilm. This is one of the greatest collections of state newspapers in the United States. Staffers are most cooperative to researchers. The Society's publication, the *Missouri Historical Review,* frequently reprints similar items from newspapers, often with a more historical rather than humorous approach. Special thanks also go to the Missouri Press Association and member newspapers for their support of my research through the years.

No individual can produce a book without special assistance, such as the support one receives from his family. Especially helpful here was the patience of my wife, Myrtle, who tolerated the many hours I spent in the State Historical Society library and on the computer. She also served as a copyeditor, noting errors and offering recommendations. And to my grandson Mike for his helpful advice in manipulating a computer. Also assisting in computer instruction was Brenda Christen of the Missouri Press Association.

Always encouraging has been the continued support of the Missouri Press Association, its director Doug Crews, and its member newspapers.

But thanks most of all to those pioneers who put their words into type, often hand-set a letter at a time, and thus brought history alive today.

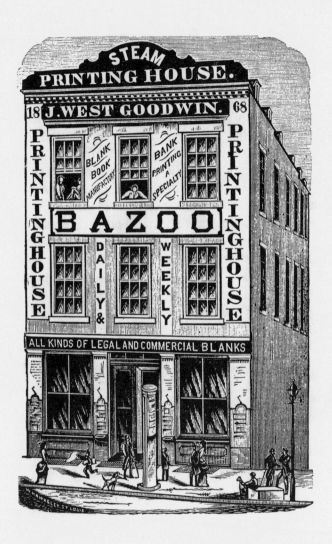

Contents

Preface

This book's goal is to provide amusement and education for those who enjoy reading past items that remind them of situations today. In compiling this book, I've stuck to the editors' creed: "make them laugh, make them cry, make them mad, just don't make them yawn."

The majority of these items, from several hundred Missouri newspapers, paint a picture of the mid-America of the past. They represent the voices of many editors, whose wit and wisdom touched topics of concern then, that may remind you of similar incidents, individuals or events in your own life.

James L. Wilcox, editor of the *Ashland Bugle* from 1877 to 1940, printed thousands of paragraphs; many were widely copied in newspapers throughout Missouri and beyond. Wilcox represented his era: He "solicited all the news and advertising, wrote editorials, gathered in subscribers, set the type by hand, did the press work, mailed out or otherwise delivered the papers and swept out the office. His editorial quips have been widely copied. He, like many other country editors, was a philosopher and a witty person. He seldom wrote out his copy, but would get his news or ideas for editorials and go to the type case and set the material, one letter at a time, ready to be printed" (from the *Ashland Area Business Directory,* produced by the Ashland Area Chamber of Commerce, Ashland, Mo., 1993).

Wilcox's writings do not follow today's "politically correct" philosophy. Obviously those editors did not concern themselves with libel laws. Their readers anticipated the weekly editions and looked forward to such pithy paragraphs. In the majority of instances, the original writers' names were lost in history. And probably many paragraphs credited to specific newspapers came from other publications.

On the other hand, some editors prized their comments, as the *Adrain Journal* noted in 1889: "The *Schell City News* and the *Foster News* both copied an article in the *Journal* last week and never gave us credit for it. It was the only original article we ever wrote, gentlemen, and that's why we are kicking." Some editors, apparently to calm their conscience, would identify such paragraphs with EX, short for Exchange. In decades past, the small-town editor usually obtained much of his material from "exchanges," normally publications in nearby communities.

These pioneer editors seldom, if ever, expected to achieve a fortune in the newspaper business. In 1901, the editor of the *Maryville Nodaway Forum,* noted: "Few men get rich editing a country newspaper. But then every man ought to devote a part of his life to the service of the Creator and the betterment of mankind, and what better way is there than that of publishing a Democratic newspaper?" Politics played a significant role. In fact, many publications were founded to support a major political party. Under such circumstances, the publisher expected the party to support him in return, through job printing and subscriptions.

Some editors must have feared being too free with their comments; rather, they produced predominately news-oriented factual publications, most useful for today's historians and genealogists, yet often dull to read. In Sikeston, the *Standard* in 1919 reported that its editor "prefers to express his views on the things that he believes will be good for the country and the community in which he lives and he never stops to consider whether it will suit everybody or not."

A new publisher would offer a Salutory in his first edition. Such men (and in those days only men were involved in such publications) were optimistic. For example, the founder of the *Glasgow Journal* in 1868 wrote about "high hopes and bright expectations of doing good for ourself, and for the people among whom we have cast our lot. In entering upon the discharge of our duty as an editor, we do so with a knowledge of the responsibilities and labor attended to it. We conform to the custom of presenting a brief statement of the course we shall pursue. Promises die like pie crusts, too often made to be broken. We would prefer our paper to speak for itself. . . ."

When Ed Watson became the editor and proprietor of the *Columbia Tribune* in 1905, he promised that his newspaper would "endeavor to perform the cardinal functions of a newspaper—the upbuilding and advancement of the community in which it is published ... a newspaper for all people." Similar comments may be found in hundreds of Missouri newspapers that have appeared since the first was published here in 1808, called the *Missouri Gazette*, in St. Louis. They seldom mentioned humor as a goal, but longtime journalists overcame the monotony of routine news by offering their opinions in editorials and humorous wordplay.

This book is not a history of Missouri newspapers. This has been recorded in two previous volumes by the author, *Missouri Newspapers* (University of Missouri Press, 1964) and *Missouri Newspapers and the Missouri Press Association: 125 Years of Service, 1867-1992* (Heritage House, 1992). It does, however, record the more humorous and at times philosophical approach to reporting newsworthy subjects through short paragraphs. They were timely and provided earthly advice for readers, much as Ben Franklin had performed with his newspapers and almanacs.

Politicians received many pointed arrows. But the most frequent challenges for comments usually involved men and women and their relationship, along with the problems associated with younger folks. Keep in mind that these editors were men, and the majority of the readers were men. There are occasions when women are not always treated as 20th-Century women's organizations prefer today. Nevertheless, editors often praised their efforts. A few even predicted the advances women have recorded since.

Some terms and comments may not be clearly understood by today's readers. In early years an individual subscribed to a newspaper generally without any advance payment. After he became delinquent, he often sought to discontinue the paper. But the publisher would not stop the paper until the individual had paid all arrears (overdue debts). This, apparently, was an early Catch-22. During depression times, the publisher would accept produce and other items in lieu of money, which he knew he wouldn't receive under any condition. Thus one reads of chickens, eggs, wood and other items accepted on payments.

While there were numerous examples of editors "fighting with words" with other editors, mostly those nearby or in the same community would get together at the Missouri Press Association and/or regional press groups' conventions to share comments about newspapering and to socialize. There were more family-owned newspapers then. Frequently one generation continued what an early one had started, such as the Blantons in Sikeston, Shelbina and Paris; the Whites in Mexico; and others such as the Aull family in Lamar. The current publisher of the *Democrat* there wrote that the family's style then was "tell it all" journalism "no matter who it hurts." Yet, he added, "the community knew they had the community's best interests at heart and they were trusted to tell the truth. They also always upheld the community."

There was a closer relationship in "those days" between the editor and his community. He was a member of that town, not a representative of an absentee owner. His future rested with the growth of the community. If it grew, so did his newspaper. It if failed, so did his publication. And he was able to "joke" with his readers, since he was acquainted with most of them, their families and their backgrounds.

While using humor to attract readers, these editors often used similar enticements to gain community support for worthwhile projects. And when individual names were omitted in editorial comments, no doubt many readers were well aware of the targets of an editor's pointed remarks.

And as individuals read these old-time comments today, the more they become aware of how frequently similar problems continue throughout the ages. Complaints about today's congressmen and women and the state legislators, as well as local political leaders, were often treated with rather direct suggestions from the editors about what they should have done or reminded of "bad things" they had performed.

Today there are a few such newspaper paragraphers. The *Kansas City Star*'s Bill Tammeus represents one of the best. His paragraphs center around current topics. His comments help us to avoid getting too alarmed or too worried about the activities, or lack of activity, of our politicians. Most anyone can write a column about a topic; only a few writers can successfully condense such material into a succinct paragraph that readers will enjoy and remember.

This book, then, reflects what readers were exposed to decades ago. When copies of older newspapers are available in one's community, one should take the time to re-read them. The past will come alive and the reader will realize how fortunate they are to be living in today's world, despite its many problems.

William H. Taft
Professor Emeritus
School of Journalism
University of Missouri-Columbia

Introduction

Bill Taft, who quilted this book over several years of eye-stressing work, started giving me assignments 30-plus years ago when he was one of my professors at the University of Missouri School of Journalism (an institution that has survived both of us in reasonably decent shape). And he hasn't quit yet.

Which is why I'm writing this introduction and not, say, someone with a Ph.D.—someone renowned in academia for his or her astounding knowledge of the ancient (as these things go) art of newspaper paragraphing.

Professor Taft, for reasons perhaps not even clear to him, has decided that paragraphs written years ago by Missouri country editors are still worth reading today. It does not surprise me that he is right about this, for it turns out, much to my surprise (and the surprise of my parents, who had much higher hopes for me), that I am a Missouri paragrapher. Taft is, in fact, serendipitously and almost brilliantly right about the value of re-reading old paragraphs. This collection proves it—containing, as it does, some precious gems.

There was a time in my life when I never imagined that anyone would ever bother to collect or study the newspaper paragraph (the way, say, butterflies or fungi are collected and studied). But in 1979, a couple of years after I fell (or got pushed) into the paragraphing business for the *Kansas City Star,* I ran across a fellow from Greeley, Colorado, named Walter Stewart, who may or may not have been gainfully employed in academia or worse. I don't recall.

Stewart told me he was putting together a book of sorts on the paragraph genre and wanted to know what I knew about the subject. Why, hardly anything, I told him, except that I have to write 13 of them for publication every working day and that some days it is not too difficult and some days I would rather be putting fenders on Fords or cleaning the Aegean stables, if the Aegeans had any openings.

Stewart, whose later whereabouts (if any) I have lost, left in my possession a thick draft of his book, which, for all I know, was either never published or was published and spent 12 years on the *New York Times* best-seller list. I am simply too busy writing paragraphs to keep track of such things. (The surprise is that for all these years I've kept track of Stewart's manuscript. In fact, I keep it in my Aegean stable. Next to my Ford.)

My point in even dragging the completely innocent Walter Stewart into this is that at the start of Chapter One in his book Stewart quotes one

Rufus Terral (a likely name) on the nature of the newspaper paragraph. Despite his name, Rufus Terral was absolutely right about the essence of the paragraph: "A piece of editorial ordnance . . . a spitball lovingly fired out of a rubber band, a tack placed thoughtfully in a chair." Well, almost right. He should have said "on a chair," but let it go.

Bill Vaughan, my extraordinarily gifted predecessor at the *Star,* once noted that there was a time in our country's history when newspaper paragraphers roamed the land. They were as plentiful as buffalo. This would have been back when the limited attention span of today's readers didn't require that newspaper stories be reduced to three paragraphs and a pie chart. But today I could attend a paragraphers convention alone and have a quorum. Columnists today are a much more diverse breed—as evidenced by the membership of the National Society of Newspaper Columnists (which, however much it might want to, cannot deny I was once its president). Some specialize in nothing but stocks and bonds. Some in gardening or bridge. Some in fields so narrow you can't even major in the subject in college.

With so many columnists writing about such limited subjects, I suppose we could argue about who today is filling the honorable generalist role of the newspaper paragrapher (besides me, I mean). Stand-up comics? Talk show host? (Say it isn't so!) Who knows?

I know only that hurling editorial ordnance, or placing word tacks thoughtfully on chairs, is still a righteous profession with a fascinating history. And I'm glad Bill Taft cared enough to rescue some of that history for us. I'm equally glad that he isn't going to give me a test on this material next Tuesday morning. And if he intends to, he can get someone else to write this introduction.

Bill Tammeus
Kansas City Star
May 1996

It All Began in the Garden

It all began with Adam and Eve. Since that time, life continues to be exciting, challenging and confusing. Newspaper editors offered their readers many sage thoughts designed to assist them in solving their precarious balances of love between men and women, their children and their pets—not to mention the problems that all started with one bite of the apple long ago.

Romance, courtship and the "games" youth participate in were also popular matters for discussion, including the problems they encounter as they move ahead in their pursuit of happiness.

Such pioneer editors were free with their advice, frequently presenting their opinions in a humorous manner, their wisdom woven tightly around short poems or subtly concealed in stories with a moral theme. However presented, these items were widely read and widely copied by other editors.

So, let's start at the real beginning: Adam and Eve. . . .

Dress Style Set

Eve is the only woman on record who never turned around to see what the other women had on.

Hartsburg Truth, 4-10-1903

It isn't hard to convince the average married man that as soon as Eve began to think about clothes, there was an end of Paradise.

Shelbyville Shelby County Herald, 2-5-1919

While Adam had a surplus of woes, pity Eve who had a scarcity of clothes.

Ashland Bugle, 2-27-1938

Perfection Still Waits

Undoubtedly there are many men in Montrose who are mighty glad Adam wasn't perfect, seeing that the influence of heredity is so exceedingly strong within us.

Montrose Tidings, 1-6-1919

There is record of one honest, sincere man. Adam told Eve that she was the only woman in the world for him.

Ashland Bugle, 11-9-1922

Adam is mentioned in history only because he happened to be Eve's husband.

Ashland Bugle, 7-6-1922

The Role of the Apple

"Why did Adam bite the apple?" said the schoolmaster to a country boy. "Because he had no knife," said the boy.

St. Charles Missourian, 7-1-1820

"We have sacrificed our beautiful home in Eden just for an apple," exclaimed Adam. "Yes," replied Eve. "Isn't the high cost of living getting to be something terrible?"

Holden Enterprise, 6-19-1919

What's Your Verdict?

Is this a better planet then when Adam ran it?

Ashland Bugle, 1-19-1939

Love Can Be Happy or Sad

She was a sweet young thing and they had exchanged the ballroom for the conservatory. As his arm stole around her mousseline de soie waist she murmured: "Am I the first girl you ever hugged?" He was a newspaper man and therefore he could not tell a lie, so he replied: "No, sweetness, you are the third edition I have put to press tonight."

Salem Democratic Bulletin, 8-29-1901

A girl will always tell how a man made love to her when it was the other way about, and a man is just as big a liar when he tells of his string of broken hearts he has made.

Smithville Democrat-Herald, 1-2-1914

His first love and his first shave are two of the things that occur in the life of every man which he never forgets.

Skidmore Standard, 8-12-1898

Looks Ahead of Brains?

The fool man appreciates the nonsense of a pretty woman more often than he does the sense of a homely one.

Smithville Democrat-Herald, 1-2-1914

Don't Believe All You Read

When a woman has had nine children she begins to have suspicions about some of the beautiful passages in love stories.

McFall Mirror, 1-9-1903

And What Is Love?

Love is a higher intellectual exercise than hate.

Sedalia Advertiser, 9-3-1864

"Love is honey mixed with gall," says a poet. The girls furnish the honey part and the boys do the rest.

Malden Dunkin News, 6-16-1905

Love's young dream often turns out to be the married woman's nightmare.

Nevada Post, 5-4-1906

Sally Jones says that when she was in love, she felt as if she was in a tunnel, with a train of cars coming both ways.

St. Louis Sentinel, 4-28-1855

Quite a number of our young readers, male and female, are occasionally troubled to know what Love is. We find the following tolerably clever description of Love in an old magazine: "Love is like the Devil, because it torments us; like Heaven, because it wraps the soul in bliss; like salt because it is relishing; like pepper because it often sets one on fire; like sugar, because it is sweet; like a rope, because it is often the death of a man; like prison, because it can make one miserable; like wine, because it makes one happy; like a man, because it is here today and gone tomorrow; like a woman, because there is no getting rid of it; like a beacon, because it glides one into a bog; like a fierce courser, because it often runs away with one; like a pony, because it ambles nicely with one; like a bite of a mad dog or the kiss of a pretty woman, because they both make a man run mad; like a goose because it is silly; like a rabbit, because there is nothing like it; in a word it is like a ghost because it is like everything and like nothing—often talked about, but never seen, touched or understood."

Columbia Missouri Statesman, 8-5-1864

That Love Letter and Action

In order that a love letter may be what it should be, one should begin it without knowing what he is going to say, and end it without knowing what he has said.

Hardin News, 2-27-1902

A young man who was caught straining his sweetheart to his bosom the other night, justified himself on the ground that he has a right to straining his own honey.

Versailles Gazette, 6-3-1871

Still True, 175 Years Later?

Virtue wants more admirers. Wisdom more supplicants. Truth more real friends. Honesty more practitioners. . . . Love, Charity and our Banks want to be in better credit. Every old bachelor wants a wife, and every girl of sixteen a husband.

Franklin Missouri Intelligencer, 9-25-1819

Whoever looks for a friend without imperfections will look in vain. With all our faults we love ourselves and we ought to be fair-minded enough to love our friends in the same manner.

Sikeston Standard, 2-2-1917

Just Wait and Listen

Cure for Love—Hide in a closet and listen to a conversation between a couple who have been married a year, while they think themselves unheard.

Hannibal True American, 2-15-1855

Prescription for Success

Hints on Love Making:

First catch your lover. Hold him when you have him.
Don't let go of him to catch every new one that comes along.
Try to get pretty well acquainted with him before you take him for life.
Unless you intend to support him, find out whether he earns enough to
     support you.
Don't make up your mind that he is an angel.
Don't palm yourself off on him as one either.
Don't let him spend his salary on you; that right should be reserved till
     after marriage.
If you have conscientious scruples against marrying a man with a
     mother, say so in time, that he may get rid of her to oblige you,
     or get rid of you to oblige her, as she thinks best.
If you object to secret societies and tobacco, it is better to come out with
     your objections now than to reserve them for certain lectures.
If your adorer happens to fancy a certain shade of hair, don't color or
     bleach to oblige him. Remember, your hair belongs to you and
     he doesn't.
Be very sure it is the man you are in love with, and not the clothes he
     wears. Fortune and fashion are both so fickle it is foolish to take
     a stylish suit for better or worse.
If you intend to keep three servants after marriage, settle the matter
     beforehand. The man who is making love to you may expect you
     to do your own washing.   *continued*

Don't try to hurry up a proposal by carrying on a flirtation with some other fellow. Different men are made of different material, and the one you want may go off in a fit of jealousy and forget to come back.

If you have a letter to write don't copy it out of a "Letter Writer." If your young man ever happened to consult the same book, he would know your sentiments were borrowed.

Don't marry a man to oblige any third person in existence. It is your right to suit yourself in the matter. But remember at the same time that love is blind, and a little friendly advice from one whose advice is worth having may insure a lifetime of happiness or prevent one of misery.

In love affairs always keep your eyes wide open, so that when the right man comes along you may see him. When you do see him you will recognize him, and the recognition will be mutual.

If you have no fault to find with him personally, financially, conscientiously, socially, morally, politically, religiously, or any other way, he is probably perfect enough to suit you, and you can afford to—

Believe him,
Hope in him,
Love him,
Marry him.

Rockport Atchison County Journal, 1-27-1883

More Advice for Lovers

HINT TO LOVERS—If a youth is wooingly disposed towards any damsel, as he values his happiness, let him follow my advice. Call on the young lady when she least expects you, and take notice of the appearance of all that is under her control. Observe if the shoes fit neatly—if the gloves are clean and the hair neat—and I would forgive a man for breaking off an engagement, if he discovered a greasy novel hid under the cushion of a sofa, or a hole in the garniture of the prettiest foot in the world. Slovenliness will ever be avoided by a well-regulated mind as would a pestilence. A woman cannot always be dressed, particularly one in middle or humble life, when her duty, and it is consequently to be hoped her pleasure, lies in superintending and assisting in all domestic matters, but she may always be neat and well-appareled, and as certainly as a virtuous woman is a crown of glory to her husband, so surely is a slovenly one a cross of thorns.

St. Louis Missouri Argus, 8-5-1836

It is no misfortune for a nice young lady to lose her good name, if a nice young gentleman gives her a better.

Cape Girardeau Eagle, 6-21-1862

Blushing No Problem

With the prevailing fashions there should be no trouble in settling the old question as to how far down a girl blushes.

Lewistown Record, 5-13-1920

Flattery Has Its Place

Flattery makes everybody sick but those who swallow it.

Palmyra Spectator, 1-19-1866

None of us object to flattery providing we are the object of it.

St. Louis Progressive Press, 12-26-1930

Flattery is the commerce of falsehood and the food of vanity.

Richfield Monitor, 12-8-1855

Kissing Plays Major Role

The ancients believed that kissing a pretty girl was a sure cure for headaches. After all, there's nothing like the old-fashioned remedies.

Jamesport Gazette, 8-15-1905

Lots of lips just made to kiss are made over again afterwards.

Jefferson City Capital News, 1-7-1922

The girl students in a Dakota school went on strike and the professor kissed them into subjection. Would you like to be a professor?

Malden Dunkin News, 3-10-1905

Who Is the Pursuer?

Just why does one woman kiss another when so many willing men are willing to be sacrificed?

Ozark Christian County Republican, 5-12-1916

When two girls meet they kiss. When two men meet they don't. That shows who wants the kissing.

Ridgeway Journal, 4-17-1891

What passage of scripture gives the ladies authority to kiss gentlemen? Do unto others as you would others should do unto you.

Liberty Tribune, 6-27-1856

Just Follow the Fly

The latest way to secure a kiss has just come to light by a yarn-spinner in one of our exchanges. He says, "I was sitting in the parlor with my best girl when an idea struck me, and worked all right. I gazed at the ceiling a moment, and then announced that I saw a fly and while her face was turned upward I kissed her rose bud mouth, and she caught on and it wasn't a minute until she saw another fly, then another and another, until she protested the entire top of the room was covered with flies."

Albany Ledger, 9-14-1894

Practice Makes Perfect

Ladies should see that these rules are strictly observed. The gentleman should be taller than the lady he intends to kiss. Take her right hand in yours and draw her gently to you, pass your left hand over her right shoulder diagonally down across her back, under her left arm; press her to your bosom, at the same time she will throw her head back and you will have nothing to do but to lean a little forward, press your lips to hers, and the thing is done. Don't make a noise about it, as if you were shooting off firecrackers, nor pounce down like a hungry hawk upon an innocent dove, but gently fold the damsel in your arm without smashing her standing collar, or spoiling her curls and with a sweet pressure on her mouth, revel in the blissfulness of your situation and without smacking your lips over it as you would over a glass of beer.

Memphis Reveille, 1-6-1866

And More Kissable Quotes

If a girl kisses a dog perhaps it's as good as she is used to.
Richmond Missourian, 11-7-1901

It is said that kissing causes freckles, but, says an exchange, every red-headed girl in the country knows better.
Richmond Conservator, 1-16-1885

Why is a kiss like a rumor? Because it goes from mouth to mouth.
Richmond Conservator, 4-6-1867

"What is a kiss?" asked a New York poetess. Is the lady from Missouri?
Hartsburg Truth, 5-10-1907

On the Road to Matrimony

Now that the editors have offered their wit and wisdom about what love is, as well as what it isn't, they now bring together the participants, the men and the women, with their varying viewpoints and outlook toward matrimony.

Upon reading the following passages, it becomes evident that men and women are not always in agreement with what constitutes the "ideal" mate, or what constitutes the "ideal" marriage. For example, they may not agree on what a kiss means, or for that matter, just how one should kiss.

On the sidelines, there are some men and women who avoid marriage, or at least attempt to make the public feel they prefer bachelorhood or being an "old Maid," a term widely used in the past that applied to an unmarried woman. Or do they? Missouri's editors were quick to share their theories on the subject.

Also in this chapter, editors offer varied approaches as to the role of the women in our society, along with comments about the men. Today's readers must remember that the great majority of these editors were men. The "Equal Rights" philosophy was slow in reaching the editorial world of newspapers.

What Is a Good Wife?

A man's idea of a good wife is one who never asked him for money and doesn't sit up for him when he is out late.

Calhoun Clarion, 7-26-1902

"Marriage," says one of the greatest of living writers, "is not the end of life." Certainly not. If he said "It is the beginning of life," he would have come nearer the truth.

Bloomfield Vindicator, 9-25-1880

Problem with Sisters

A girl might as well be retired to a convent as to have a younger sister grow up who is better looking than she is.

Albany Ledger, 12-7-1894

Let the thin sisters rejoice while they may, it's the plump old ladies who always look kind and motherly, and who get all of the nice soft talk about the beauty of old age.

Lamar Democrat, 6-10-1909

And Other Guidelines

A girl with a well located dimple looks upon life as a thing very simple.

Ashland Bugle, 1-26-1911

A woman goes to the theatre to see what's on in the boxes; a man to see what's off on the stage.

Ashland Bugle, 5-18-1911

A Missouri girl who was born on a merry-go-round has applied for membership in the Daughters of the Revolution, says an exchange.

Ashland Bugle, 6-23-1904

Paint Has Its Place

What this town needs is more paint on the place and less paint on the face.

Ashland Bugle, 8-31-1922

It costs more to paint a nose than a house, and no man thinks he can afford both, hence he lets the house go.

Fayette Howard County Advertiser, 6-21-1906

There Are "Rights" Too

Before women pine and pant to have turned over to them the affairs, heretofore dominated by men, it would be well for them to learn to hire help and get along with it.

Lamar Democrat, 4-8-1909

Where women can obtain their "rights"—at the shoemakers. Their "lefts" too.

Kirksville North Missouri Register, 12-8-1870

Joy from Shopping

Those ladies who are always shopping, but never buy anything, are called counter-irritants.

Huntsville North Missouri Herald, 2-10-1869

According to the observation of a certain unmarried man, the happiest moments in a woman's life are those spent in shopping and talking on the telephone.

Shelbina Democrat, 12-25-1935

Look Before You Leap

A young lady seeking a situation was interested in an advertisement for some one to do light housekeeping. So she wrote to the advertiser, asking where the light-house was, and if there was any way of getting to shore on Sundays.

Jefferson City People's Tribune, 12-8-1870

How many fond mothers and frugal housewives keep their pretty daughters and their preserves for some extra occasion—some "big bug" or other—until both become sour. This seems to us marvelously poor economy.

Huntsville Randolph Citizen, 5-19-1855

Dress, Age and Other Concerns

You can tell the exact age of a tree by its rings; but this rule doesn't apply in the case of a society woman.

Hartsburg Truth, 2-27-1903

A country girl coming from a morning walk was told she looked as fresh as a daisy kissed by the dew. To which she innocently replied: "You've got my name right—Daisy, but his wasn't Dew."

Jefferson City People's Tribune, 9-7-1881

A scientist authority says that woman has more backbone than man. And she shows more of it than man, too.

Louisiana Journal, 2-19-1920

We admire ladies because of their beauty, respect them for their virtue, adore them on account of their intelligence, and love them because we can't help it.

Liberty Tribune, 1-13-1882

The *Chillicothe Constitution* mourns the "passing of the good old days when a man drove a horse with one arm and supported a dainty bit of calico with the other." To which the *Nevada Post* replies: "Cheer up brother. How much greater are the joys of modern times! Now a man drive a sixty horse power runabout with his knees and uses both arms."

Concordia Concordian, 1-29-1941

When a Missouri girl can turn a batter cake without slinging it onto the stove, she is considered competent to assume the charge of a family.

Hamilton News-Graphic, 3-14-1890

"So you are going to keep house, are you?" said an elderly maiden to a young woman recently married. "Yes," was the reply. "Going to have a girl, I suppose?" was queried. The newly-made wife colored, and then quietly responded that "she did not know whether it would be a boy or a girl."

Liberty Tribune, 6-27-1856

Before the Fax Era

Did you ever see a woman get ready to write a letter? If you never did just observe the next time you get an opportunity. First she hunts around for a long time for her pen. Then she begins to search the place for ink. She has forgotten whether she left it down at the hen house, the last time she marked the eggs of the sitting hen, or whether it's in the southwest corner of the lower drawer of her dresser. Finally she fails to find it and has to send down town for a new bottle. Thus secured it's too late to write that day, but she keeps the letter on her mind and before the week is up she starts again. By that time the pen is lost, but finally she locates it around some place where the children were playing with it the day before, and then she gets busy. If she has any particular objection writing the letter, she studiously conceals it, for page after page. She writes about the weather, about her last fall suit, a hat she has just literally stolen for $7.98, the children who were there Sunday, what she had for dinner, and that the folks were well except for colds. Then after the inevitable P.S. she scrawls in a line and a half what she is driving at. She then carefully folds the missive up, addresses it and gives it to hubby to mail, right off. Three days later she finds it in the inside pocket of the coat he left at home for her to mend.

Lamar Democrat, 11-2-1905

The observing editor of the *Glasgow Times* says that short skirts do not necessarily make the woman look shorter, but they always make the man look longer.

Mokane Herald, 8-3-1910

When you see a beautiful maid sailing along the street with head in the air and seeing nothing and hearing less, it's a safe bet she is wondering what sort of a sensation she is creating.

Ozark Christian County Republican, 3-17-1916

The marriage crop is ripening very fast in our county. But we fear there will yet be some couples pulled green.

Paris Monroe County Appeal, 8-19-1881

It is in the nature for a woman to think that some ugly man is good looking.

Rocheport Commercial, 6-28-1895

All This in 1867!

We notice that Mrs. Bettie Lackey has received the appointment of Post Mistress at Jefferson City. This reminds us that the position of women is decidedly in the ascendant. There are quite a number of women now filling official positions in various parts of the country, and the question of admitting them to the right of suffrage is being seriously considered by many good and influential men. And the young, glorious, and progressive Kansas—foremost in all the leading reforms of the day, had through her Legislature, passed an act admitting the question of female suffrage to a vote of her people.

We'll bet a small sized greenback that before the expiration of ten years more, the ladies will vote everywhere in the country.

We don't wish to be understood, however, as committing ourself in favor of it. We have not yet decided on the subject! It is a ticklish matter for some men! But it does seem to us that it will be a might pleasant thing for a good-looking man to be a candidate for office when that time comes. Electioneering will pay then.

Springfield Patriot, 4-9-1867

A young lady at a ball called her beau an Indian because he was on her tail all the time.

St. Charles Cosmos, 3-25-1881

A woman sometimes prefers a man's presents to his company.

St. Louis Carondelet Progress, 12-3-1898

Don'ts for Girls

Don't, whatever the fashion may be, wear a lot of jewelry. Don't talk of your ailments in company or discuss your diseases. Don't be profuse with terms of endearment and kisses in public. Don't wear a fine gown and shabby boots. Don't have dirty nails, soiled handkerchief, or soiled linen. Don't use quantities of perfume. Don't make a point of being late for church or for any entertainment to which you may be invited. It is a habit which does not increase your importance and sensibly decreases your popularity.

St. Louis Carondelet News, 3-28-1903

Take a Number

A young woman in Chicago, who had lost her speech by a severe cold, had twenty offers of marriage in one week.

Versailles Morgan County Banner, 6-31-1867

Women have to rock something; if it isn't the cradle, it's the ship of state.

St. Louis Argus, 1-2-1925

The woman who never watched her neighbors is said to be the cousin to the woman who did not know how many dresses her sister-in-law had.

Ste. Genevieve Fair Play, 11-21-1872

Old Maids: A Dying Class?

The flapper says she only acts like an old maid thinks.

Jefferson City Capital News, 1027-1922

Motto Tells It All

A new organization called the "Old Maids' Mutual Aid" is in process of organization and will probably be launched in this city before the first of January. Next year will be Leap Year and the society proposes to take advantage of the opportunity thus offered to ladies, who, having arrived at years of discretion, are unmated and unloved. The object of the society will be to protect the members and advance their matrimonial interests. Meetings will be guarded by the usual lodge restrictions and no one will be admitted who is not an Old Maid in good standing. A large membership is secured already and new recruits will easily be found, because every day some blossoming tulip is withered by the frosts of time, relegated to the ancient and venerable class and thus eligible to membership in this society. The Record was privileged with an interview with one of the leading organizers of the society and was informed that the motto of the society will be "Anybody, Lord."

Sarcoxie Record, 12-4-1903

Fooled You, Too?

An old maid is an old woman who has not been fool enough to be fooled by every fool who has been fool enough to try to fool her.

Columbia Missouri Statesman, 6-10-1898

Keep on a Rope?

How an old maid always eyes a single gentleman: She looks at him as she does a dog in dog days—wondering whether he intends to bite.

Waverly Saturday Morning Visitor, 1-8-1859

Patience Has Its Place

Nine battles out of ten are won by patience and determination. It is almost impossible to permanently defeat the man who will not give up and who with patience goes on his way.

Sikeston Standard, 4-26-1914

Patience is a flower that does not grow in every garden.

Novinger Record, 4-27-1906

Odds and Ends—the End

When a woman has company she apologizes for everything she puts on the table, and when no one is there but her family she defends it.

St. Louis Carondelet Progress, 12-2-1898

Men: Their Habits and Problems

Some Never Change

There are some men so obstinate they would rather be kicked in the head by a mule rather than admit they had made a mistake.

Warrenton Banner, 3-23-1917

You can hide all the average man's wisdom in a pretty girl's dimple.

Lilbourn Herald, 7-10-1914

The man who takes his own time working by the day will work by the day his whole life through.

Carl Junction Graphic, 1-9-1907

Some Are Philosophical

For every man who thinks twice before he speaks there are a dozen who do not think at all.

Mendon Constitution, 1-10-1914

No man is good enough to point the finger of scorn at his neighbor.

Macon Chronicle, 2-9-1915

Measure of Success

No man ever had to stop climbing the ladder of fame because there wasn't another rung above him.

Huntsville Randolph Democrat, 1-5-1900

A man who is perfectly satisfied with himself is usually easily pleased.

Carl Junction Graphic, 1-19-1907

Too Much Noise

Men are generally like wagons—they rattle prodigiously when there is nothing in them.

Kansas City Star, 10-20-1880

A man may talk nonsense, but if he occupies a high position, it will be accepted as wisdom.

Ashland Bugle, 9-4-1919

To Thy Self Be True

"A man who'll maliciously set fire to a barn," said Mr. Slow, "and burn up twenty cows, ought to be kicked to death by a jackass, and I'd like to do it." Slow is very severe sometimes.

Fredericktown Conservative, 8-2-1861

Many a man was happier in childhood building houses of blocks than when a man and building blocks of houses.

Urich Herald, 5-4-1911

Talk about woman's vanity. Note how few the number of men who can pass a mirror set up in a public place without a smirk and a curling of the mustache and an adjustment of the neck tie.

Graham Post, 3-18-1909

Not Too Many Around

A model husband, in our opinion, is not a man who brings wealth to the home, nor one who endows his wife with a fine social position, but the one who gives to his wife the best of himself, who appreciates her virtues and pardons her faults.

Novinger Record, 5-11-1906

Man was made a little lower than the angels a good while ago and he hasn't kept up very well.

Ashland Bugle, 2-24-1921

Stages of Men Vary

Stages: Man creeps into childhood—bounds into youth—sobers into manhood—softens into age—totters into second childhood—and slumbers into the cradle prepared for him.

St. Joseph Adventure, 3-15-1850

The Six Stages: Man is at ten a child; at twenty, wild; at thirty, tame, if ever; at forty, wise; at fifty, rich; at sixty, good or never.

St. Joseph Herald, 4-17-1862

All the world's a stage, but some of the actors are enough to make any man tired of the show, observes the *Centralia Courier*.

Ashland Bugle, 6-1-1905

Anyone You Know?

Usually the man who is forever questioning the honesty of other men will bear a great deal of watching himself.

Calhoun Clarion, 6-2-1902

A man's wealth is the number of things which he loves and blesses and the number of things he is loved and blessed for.

Shelton Enterprise, 8-23-1901

Man is not a giraffe by any means, but when a pretty girl trips along, he can twist his neck in a dozen different ways.

Smithville Democrat-Leader, 1-12-1917

The man who yearns to be a boy again is quite apt to forget what a task it was to wake up from a sound sleep on the sofa and go out to the kitchen and wash his feet before he could go to bed.

Winston News, 3-17-1910

Are Men Any Wiser?

A wise man will desire no more than what he may get justly, use soberly, distribute cheerfully and leave contentedly.

Auxvasse Review, 8-12-1909

A young man who spends his time in sowing wild oats seldom becomes a member of the Old Settlers Association.

Carl Junction Graphic, 1-11-1907

A man is known by the company that refuses to keep him.

Ashland Bugle, 4-25-1918

Men are superior to women in acquiring special kinds of learning, or mastering particular lines of work. But they are not as smart as women, by any means. Very few men can manage their wives, but most any woman can easily manage her husband.

Lamar Democrat, 4-1-1909

Now That Is Slow

There is a man in a neighboring town who is so slow that his neighbors say the only thing he was ever known to catch was the measles.

Auxvasse Review, 10-6-1910

Men Compared Again

Many a man who claims to be looking for work wouldn't recognize a job if it stepped up and tapped him on the shoulder.

Hartsburg Truth, 12-25-1903

Too many of the men who are waiting for their ships to come in do their waiting where they can see the schooners crossing the bar, according to Luke McLake.

Hartsburg Truth, 12-10-1915

The prodigal son is the young man who loses everything except his way home.

Ashland Bugle, 3-31-1910

It is a fine theory that the greatest man on earth is one's self and that his biggest enemy is the same person.

Jefferson City Western Messenger, 2-6-1914

The man who starts throwing stones will always be surprised to discover how much of his own house is made of glass.

Lamar Democrat, 7-17-1902

Did He Get It?

"It does seem to me, Maria, as if you grow more foolish every day of your life." "Oh, no, Edward. I am a great deal wiser now than when I married you."

Huntsville Herald, 1-17-1894

A chap who thinks he is cute is never much account until he gets over that.

Richmond Missourian, 1-16-1919

Unlike the Camel

It is said that a camel can work seven days without taking a drink. In that it is just the opposite of some men who can drink seven days without doing a stroke of work.

Sikeston Standard, 9-18-1914

How to Stand High

It's not a better home we need for man. It's a better man we need for home, said someone.

Ashland Bugle, 5-16-1918

If a man will observe what he sees he will pay less attention to what he hears, and, perhaps, that will apply to women, too.

Carl Junction Graphic, 1-9-1907

Matrimony:
A Dangerous Journey?

E ditors were extremely free in their advice to those plotting a trip on the road to matrimony. While they frequently favored the men over the women, they were not adverse from time to time to criticize their own sex.

One assumes many of these comments were of the tongue-in-cheek variety, the editor no doubt having some local man or woman in mind. Reading these words today might take on a different meaning from the original views. Still, many of these items provide endearing warning signals, even decades after they were originally composed.

A common trait of country editors, these "paragraphers" generally had a lighter approach to a serious situation. See if you agree.

All Covered in Your Home?

I want you, my young sinners, to kiss and get married. . . .
Then let your homes be well provided with such comforts and
necessities as piety, pickles, pots and kettles, brushes, brooms,
benevolence, bread, charity, cheese, crackers, faith, floor, affection, cider, sincerity, onions, integrity, vinegar, virtue, wine and
wisdom. Have all these always on hand, and happiness will be
with you. Don't drink anything intoxicating—eat moderately—go
about business after breakfast—lounge a little after dinner—chat
after quarreling, and all the joy, the peace and the bliss the earth
can afford shall be yours.

Springfield Advertiser, 5-28-1844

Like Today's Soap Opera

Once upon a time the hero and the heroine in the story failed to get
married in the last chapter and lived happily ever after.

Willow Springs News, 5-2-1935

A wise wife conceals nothing from her husband—except her own faults.

Union Republican-Tribune, 1-10-1919

Merely Planning Ahead

A man in Liberty, Mo., purchased a lot in the cemetery and presented it to his wife as a Christmas present. The man is at liberty but it seems strange that he remains so.

Tarkio Atchison County World, 1-1-1903

A newspaper epigrammatist: "Every wife is the architect of her husband." Then she shouldn't be too severe on the edifice when she botches the job.

Hallsville Eagle, 7-10-1903

Courtship: Game or What?

Glancing at the daily papers we are inclined to believe a lot of women think more of catching a man than they do of holding him.

St. Clair Chronicle, 4-21-1927

If you would be happy, keep your eyes wide open during courtship and half closed after marriage.

Pleasant Hill Local, 12-17-1909

It is called courtship because it is run on rocks, often ends in a wreck, may be a transport of joy, leads you through wedlock and brings you to squalls.

Auxvasse Review, 7-20-1911

Want to Annoy Him? Or Her?

When a woman wants to annoy her husband she informs him that she is going to clean house.

Parma Victor, 7-16-1908

After a man is married, he is only willing to share the hammock with his cigar and newspaper.

Plattsburg Clinton County Democrat, 7-25-1907

If a woman has more sense than her husband she is foolish if she lets him know.

Parma Victor, 7-16-1908

Ladies who have a disposition to punish their husbands, should bear in mind that a little warm sunshine will melt an icicle much sooner than a regular north-easter.

Huntsville Randolph Citizen, 7-26-1855

Share and Share Alike

A writer in the *Kansas City Post* says: "The right to marry should imply the right to unmarry or divorce." Not at all. Marriage is not a private contract. The public has an interest. The care of children and many other conditions affect society at large. Each divorce is a public damage. Permanence of marriage is the foundation of good society. Faith in man and woman breeds honor, truth and virtue. Unfaith breeds the opposite. Nothing but the most serious situation should ever bring divorce. Let people be careful how they marry, and then abide by the consequences, until the consequences are endurable.

Plattsburg Leader, 1-31-1913

Don'ts for Husbands: Don't kill the love of a devoted woman by so-called innocent flirtation. Don't forget that your wife has a right to a regular allowance which she can call her own. Don't interfere in household matters. That is your wife's department and you know little or nothing about it.

Galena Stone County News, 4-23-1903

Really That Desperate?

True but melancholy. We have it from good authority that the girls in some parts are so hard up for husbands that they sometimes take up with lawyers and quack doctors.

Fayette Boon's Lick Times, 2-24-1844

A Chicago man killed his wife and himself because she wouldn't take a lake trip with him. This should serve as a warning to other women whose husbands want to give up their household cares for awhile and have a good time.

Hardin News, 9-12-1901

They tell us that matches are made in heaven, but somehow they never smell that way when you strike them.

St. Charles Clarion, 1-26-1881

Want to Take a Chance?

There never was a pretty girl so stupid that she couldn't fool the cleverest man of her acquaintance.

Carl Junction Graphic, 1-5-1907

There are more rooster-pecked wives than hen-pecked husbands.

Hallsville Eagle, 5-30-1903

War or Peace?

Too often marriage consists of a perpetual tug of war between opposing selfishness.

Auxvasse Review, 5-26-1910

A woman is always waiting for a husband. If she is single, she is waiting for him to propose, and if married she is waiting for him to come home.

Auxvasse Review, 6-17-1909

It's sometimes difficult for a girl to find her ideal man, but she's nearly always willing to accept a substitute.

Marshall Saline Citizen, 11-9-1898

Prepare for "His" Future

It should be the aim of every man to leave enough money with which to set up his wife's second husband in business.

Eldon Advertiser, 12-20-1894

Nice Try at Least

"Only twenty?" "Yes," she explained. "George made me promise when we were married that I would never change. I was twenty then, and mean to keep my promise."

Kansas City Star, 10-13-1880

Keeps Quiet, Too

A Los Angeles woman carries the ashes of her husband around with her in a bag, thus being always able to know where he is at nights.

Lathrop Monitor-Herald, 2-21-1907

What a Spender!

A miser in New York is willing to marry if he can find a woman sufficiently economical. He proposes that to any woman who will be his lawful wife and legal spouse he will give her lodging and board, and on every third day he will give her five cents for spending money.

Chillicothe Constitution, 2-8-1891

A girl might get a rich husband and a poor one at the same time.

Ashland Bugle, 1-18-1917

Across the Stage They Move

The Five Stages: At seventeen she said: "I want a man who is ardent in all of his love ways and whose passionate devotion may never flay. He must be tall, broad shouldered and handsome, with dark, flashing soulful eyes, and, if need be, go to the end of the world for my sake." At 20 she said: "I want a man who unties the tender sympathy of a woman with the bravery of a lion. I don't mind him being a little dissipated because that always adds a charm. He must be, however, accomplished to the last degree and capable of any sacrifice for my sake." At 25 she said: "I want a man who unites with an engaging personality a complete knowledge of the world, and if he happens to have a past he must also have a future, a man with whom I can trust myself . . . if at all times without the slightest embarrassment." At 30 she said: "I want a man with money. He can have any attributes that a man ought to possess, but he must have money and the more he has the better I will like it." At 35 she said: "I want a man."

Hartsburg Truth, 6-26-1903

Stage marriages are like stage sets: they don't last long and they are repeated many times.

Lamar Democrat, 5-28-1903

Keep the Home Fires Burning

It keeps wives as busy providing for the inner man as it does husbands providing things for the outer woman.

Buffalo Reflex, 2-20-1913

An absconding wife is thus pathetically appealed to in a "Person" column: "Jane, your absence will ruin all. Think of the children, your parents, your husband. Return. Return, all may yet be well. At any rate, enclose the key to the cupboard where the gin is."

Brookfield Gazette, 8-28-1869

Some girls think they have to be fast to catch a husband.

Jefferson City Capital News, 1-18-1922

Advice Best to Follow

Young men should never lose presence of mind, in a trying situation, says the *Elmira Advertiser*. When you take the girl you love to a picnic, and you wander away together to commune with nature, and she suddenly exclaims: "Oh, George, there's an ant down my back!" don't stand still with your mouth open, don't faint, don't go for the girl's mouth, go for the ant.

Columbia Missouri Statesman, 3-17-1882

A husband at home is worth two in a saloon.

Clinton Advocate, 7-3-1885

Did He Pay for Ad?

A husband thus announces the departure of his wife from "bed and board":

"My wife, Anne Maria, has been strayed or stolen. Whoever returns her will get his head broke. As for trusting her any body can do as they see fit—for as I never pay my own debts, it is not at all likely that I will lay awake nights thinking about other people's."

Hannibal True American, 3-15-1855

Dancing in the Dark

A few nights ago a gentleman who had just undressed and prepared for bed, blew out the lamp on the table and was groping his way across the room, when feeling for the bed his toe struck something cold and pliant. The thing seemed to open its mouth as the gentleman put the weight of his foot upon it and he jerked up his foot in double quick time, while the thing held its hold and dangled from his toe. There was a lively dancing around the darkened room and the man made a lively racket with his mouth til he succeeded in slinging the thing across the room. Then he jumped up on a table and stood there until he could light a lamp. Over near where the thing had struck the wall he saw his wife's wire spring bustle lying on the floor. He kicked himself a few times and went to bed but his wife kept awake for an hour laughing at him.

Bowling Green Times, 5-24-1888

To Flirt or Not to Flirt

The first question an honorable man asks when he sees a girl flirting is whether she is a respectable girl or not. You see how it raises the doubt at once. This being the case no modest girl can afford to indulge in this pastime with strangers. When the down is brushed from the peach the beauty is so marred that it can never be restored, and so when a girl throws lightly aside that sweet and modest reserve so becoming a maiden, she loses her greatest charm and becomes rather common and cheap. Flirting may seem to the giddy and thoughtless girl to be wonderfully amusing and she may even get an idea she is quite fascinating but it is a degrading pastime and should be frowned upon by every young lady who has an ambition to be a worthy and charming woman.

Sikeston Standard, 11-9-1914

Depends on Point of View

A clever female French writer says women should not sit beside the man they wish to conquer, but opposite him. "Attack a heart by full front, not by profile," is her expression.

St. Louis Missouri Argus, 12-11-1835

And His Qualifications?

A Wife Wanted—A Lady who possesses an ordinary share of good sense, who has had a liberal education, who has not corrupted the mind with too much novel reading, who has somewhat expanded the imagination with a moderate course of proper history, who is adept in plain needle work, who is acquainted with the duties of the kitchen as well as to decorate a drawing room, whose bosom glows with becoming warmth, whose sensorium is so happily organized as not to be moved by extremes upon trivial or common occurrences, & who is not too fond of visiting, would obtain an answer by a line to A. B. Franklin.

Missouri Intelligencer, 12-3-1819

All's Well That Ends Well

EXTEMPORANEOUS MARRIAGE—A somewhat matrimonial alliance occurred at Sigel, Missouri, the other day. A gentleman of that place was engaged to a young lady, the wedding day was fixed and the guests arrived. A few days before the nuptials were to have been solemnized, the father and brother of the bridegroom, by threats of disinheritance, persuaded him to disappoint the expectant bride, and make himself invisible in the vicinity. The evening came and at the appointed time the wedding guests collected at the house of the bride's mother, but the faithless swain did not make his appearance. An hour passed, and the bride and her friends were overwhelmed with embarrassment and mortification. When all hope of a wedding had vanished, a young gentleman of the party, being captivated with the beauty of the bride, and desirous that the company should not be disappointed, proposed, was accepted, and the couple were accordingly married. The guests were astonished and delighted and the bride and groom looked exceedingly happy.

Versailles Morgan County Banner, 5-25-1867

Long Ago, Thus Forgotten

A clergyman says that he was one day called down into his study to perform the marriage ceremony for a couple in middle life. "Have you ever been married before?" asked the clergyman of the bridegroom. "No, sir." "Have you?" to the bride. "Well, yes, I have" replied the bride,

---

laconically, "but that was 20 years ago, and he fell off a barn and killed himself when we'd been married only a week, so he really ain't worth mentioning."

Hume Border Telephone, 10-5-1901

Warning: Better Look Ahead

A man who lets his wife chop the stove-wood will not have to wear an overcoat in the more or less sweet beyond.

Richmond Missourian, 7-25-1901

The girl who can't cook (and don't want to) should look before she leaps into the married frying pan.

Richmond Missourian, 1-16-1919

Owning an automobile and getting married are something alike. It costs something to get married and it costs to own an automobile. But in both cases it costs to keep the thing going.

Aurora Advertiser, 4-24-1908

Children Have Their Place

E ditors look upon children as one of their favorite topics, one that comes the nearest to having universal appeal to readers of all ages and types. The writers were well aware that both good and bad incidents occurred in the lives of the children; they also were aware that there were both good and bad children.

So, many of these items were warnings. Editors warned not only the children but their parents about the gossipers and the "reformers." And about the dangers of being prejudiced. Or about lying. These editors emphasized the need for patience and for the development of the mind.

Interestingly, the majority of these "suggestions" apply equally well today as they did when originally printed in newspapers.

Children Have Their Place

The laughter of a little child, as a medium of cheer, is only surpassed by the sunshine and flowers.
Fayette Howard County Advertiser, 1-25-1906

No other living thing is so slow as a boy on an errand.
Grandy Miner, 2-21-1874

Children grow bad for the want of somebody to tell them how good they are. And men and women also are in the same boat. Then let us praise each other, since praise stimulates noble deeds.
Rock Port Sun, 2-2-1882

And More Advice for Living

Sensible people do not permit their heads to be turned by a crank.
Lewistown Record, 7-15-1920

It takes very little to swell some heads.
Lamar Democrat, 6-12-1909

True happiness consists principally in forgiving and forgetting.
Urich Herald, 8-10-1911

A good memory is valuable and so is a good forgetory.
Ashland Bugle, 5-12-1910

Some Family Connections

After a woman has fallen in love with the first grandchild, she becomes more reconciled to the fact that her daughter has a husband.
Harrisonville Cass County Leader, 4-19-1906

When children who are born with silver spoons in their mouth grow up there is seldom anything of them left but the spoon.
St. Joseph Weekly Herald, 5-1-1862

Seek Right Direction

It is a good policy to look ahead if you are headed in the wrong direction.
Marthasville Record, 5-14-1915

Idle people spend too much time on 'phones.
Tuscumbia Miller County Autogram, 3-27-1908

When you are sure you're right, go ahead, but don't expect the crowd to follow you.
Ashland Bugle 2-17-1910

Eat less and breathe more, talk less and think more, ride less and walk more, clothe less and bathe more, worry less and work more, waste less and give more, preach less and practice more.
Ashland Bugle, 3-22-1917

Genius Has Its Place

A genius is a man who tries to borrow money—and gets it.
Neosho Miner and Mechanic, 7-8-1910

There is no genius in life like the genius of energy and industry.
West Plains Journal, 12-8-1898

Definitions Somewhat Varied

An old lady describes a genius as "a man who knows more'n he can find out, and spills vittals on his clothes."
Sedalia Bazoo, 4-6-1873

A wit, being asked what the word genius meant, replied: "If you had it in you, you would not ask the question, but as you have not, you will never know what it means."
Columbia Missouri Intelligencer, 7-30-1831

Beware of Those Who Gossip

The geese believed that wild geese in passing over countries where there were danger of being caught by eagles, were accustomed to take small stones in their mouths to prevent their chattering and thus attracting the attention of the eagles. This might be imitated, with profit, by human prattlers. When they get into dangerous company let them remember to put a weight on their tongues.
Carrollton Journal, 11-16-1877

For every tongue of gossip there must be at least two ears.
Auxvasse Review, 5-28-1908

The man with his ear to the ground may hear more than other people, but the trouble is he hears too much that is not so.
Hallsville Eagle, 7-31-1903

How to Prevent Gossip

The gossip you hear about others is a poor thing with which to burden the mind.
Carl Junction Graphic, 1-8-1907

Gossips are people who believe twice as much as they hear.

Lilbourn Herald, 7-30-1914

The *Hale Leader* says the trouble with many people in his town is their heads are too weak to hold their tongue.

Marceline Journal, 7-21-1904

People gossip much more about vice than they do about virtue.

Ashland Bugle, 4-21-1921

Can Lead to Slander

The best way to treat slander is to let it alone and say nothing about it.

Savannah North-West Democrat, 7-12-1836

Definition of "bearing false witness against your neighbor" was given by a little girl in school. She said it was when nobody did nothing, and somebody went and told it.

St. Joseph Weekly Herald, 6-12-1836

Another Gossip Definition

The *Richmond Missourian* defines gossip: Gossip is human voice with eagle wings and a voice like a fog horn. It can be heard from Dan to Bersheba and has caused more trouble than all the bedbugs, flies, ticks, fleas, mosquitoes, grasshoppers, clinch bugs, rattlesnakes, smallpox, yellow fever, rats, blizzards, earthquakes and even whiskey than this great universe knows or will know when he shuts up shop and begins to take final invoice. In other words, it has war and Hades in a corner yelling for ice water.

Cabool Enterprise, 7-27-1906

A Great "Anti-" Drive

The ladies of Springfield, Mo., have taken rather an advanced step in the way of social reform, says the *Yellville Echo*. Through the influence of some of the leading ladies of the city, a society known as the Anti-Gossip Society has been formed. In order to become a member of the society one must take a solemn obligation "to speak no evil of any woman, whether such report be true or not." There are other localities besides Springfield that could be very greatly relieved and benefited if, not only the women, but the men as well, could be induced to enter, and adhere strictly to the obligations of such a society. The professional gossiper is the bane and curse of society everywhere. The tattler or talebearer is the synonym of a common liar, is coalesced with the devil and is in league with hell. The man or woman who is constantly "sticking their lip" into the private affairs of others meddling where they have no earthly business are the most contemptible characters that ever disgraced our world.

Pierce City Empire, 2-22-1900

Children Need Confidence

Confidence imparts a wondrous inspiration to its possessor.

Union Star Pinhook News, 5-3-1911

The noblest gift which one can offer to another is confidence.

Cole Camp Courier, 10-10-1901

Your Mind Has Its Place

If you would be useful, improve your time and cultivate your mind.

Savannah North-West Democrat, 8-9-1856

Narrowness of mind is often the cause of obstinacy; we do not easily believe beyond what we see.

Fayette Missouri Intelligencer, 1-29-1826

Tongue Control Essential

More the tongue flows, less the head knows.

Ashland Bugle, 8-25-1938

All want speech free, but don't want to listen to thee.

Ashland Bugle, 10-3-1940

A man fears a woman's tears as much as he fears her tongue.

Auxvasse Review, 2-23-1911

Satan, they say, finds work for the idle hands to do, also frequently for busy tongues.

Marthasville Record, 2-12-1915

Perpetual Motion Example

Some people are good imitations of perpetual motion. Their tongues begin running in the early morning and never slacken the pace until sleep overcomes them at night. But that is not all. While in the land of dreams their tongues absorb most of the energy of the body in order to be ready for action the next day. And so it continues from day to day and year to year, until the Lord takes pity on the rest of us and calls them home—for what purpose we don't know.

Wyaconda News-Herald, 9-13-1923

Prejudice Always Dangerous

The smallest thing in the world is prejudice and of it that's all some people have.

Ashland Bugle, 11-14-1912

It is a good time now during the revival for some of us church members that pretend to believe that Jesus arose from the dead, to prove it by showing that we are imbred with the forgiving spirit which He manifested during His life, instead of the narrow contracted prejudice by which most of us are actuated.

Belton Herald, 11-10-1894

Beware of Reformers

Quite a lot of reformers seem to think that the only way to make the world better is to make it uncomfortable.

Marthasville Record, 2-12-1915

It is often the corrupt man that speaks loudest of reform.

Ashland Bugle, 6-9-1904

Family Life a Frequent Topic

F amily life can, of course, be exciting. As we've established in the past four chapters, editors were never short on advice. Editors found the topic of family life to be another endless source for articles, at times pointing to the father and at other times to the mother with "suggestions" for improvements in the activities of both groups.

One must keep in mind that the majority of these topics appeared in the newspaper prior to television, radio and other detracting elements. In order to maintain a Christian-like family, the editors spoke about problems that follow too much drinking, too much attention to fashions and styles, and to the possibility of divorce and death.

And as we'll see, farmers, too, have their happiness and sorrows as they tend to their chores, their animals, their neighbors, and, of course, their own families.

Life Can Be Exciting

Some children are spoiled in their raising because that is the easiest way to raise them.

Mendon Constitution, 1-10-1914

Unless the child goes beyond the parent there is no progress.

Ashland Bugle, 10-5-1939

Let's Hope They Never Do

Most of men's troubles come through women. Most of women's troubles come through men. Looks like they'd let each other alone.

Lamar Democrat, 6-3-1909

And a Little Advice

Most people like to boast of their ancestors but seem to forget to live so their descendants can conscientiously do the same thing.

Aurora Advertiser, 9-17-1909

Plan for Big Events

If you wish to be happy for a day, get well shaved; if for a week, get invited to a wedding; if for a month, buy a good nag; if for half a year, buy a handsome house; if for a year, marry a handsome wife—but if would be always gay and cheerful, practice temperance and pay the printer.

Glasgow Times, 10-26-1848

Problems Really Differ

A child, like a letter, often goes astray through being badly directed.

Weston Border Times, 2-16-1864

When a girl ceases to be confidential with her mother she is then within easy reach of the devil.

Richmond Missourian, 11-7-1901

Some children are forced to believe that home is the place where all the growling is done.

Novinger Record, 6-8-1906

It must be interesting to a child to hear a father tell of his boyish pranks just after he has whipped it for some mischief.

Auxvasse Review, 6-3-1909

For a Better Farm Life

The men who make the most money from farming are not the ones who work the hardest or the most hours, but those who manage with the greatest wisdom.

Cassville Republican, 7-10-1890

Among the yellow perils that deserved attention, the dandelion should not be carelessly overlooked.

Jamesport Gazette, 7-4-1905

Before Ag Schools, Too

An English farmer recently remarked that "he fed his land when it was hungry; rested it when it was weary, and weeded it before it was foul." Seldom, if ever, was so much agricultural wisdom condensed in a single sentence.

Lancaster Excelsior, 3-29-1866

No farmer is successful who thinks more of his barn than he does of his house. The most beautiful fact in the farmer's work is that everything he plants is a lesson in faith. Farming is as old as the human race and is yet in its infancy.

Lilbourn Herald, 8-31-1914

Better Farm Care Needed

There is a great deal of land, chiefly profitable for timber purposes, which exists in each state and which ought to be taken possession of by right of eminent domain, if the interests of the country are to be properly protected; but the government can adopt a forest policy only for lands that have not yet passed out of its hands.

Drexel Star, 10-6-1892

Around and Around He Goes

A Kansas man has a row of corn 25 miles long. He began a 50-acre field as a continuous circle, his object being to attain a curiosity, but he found that his long row was a time-saver, as there was no turning at the ends of the row.

Calhoun Clarion, 11-15-1902

Suckers Then Too

A farmer near Macon is the easiest mark on record. He was awakened the other night by men pounding on his door. They said they were hauling a hog past his place and the hog jumped out into his hog lot. They asked him to catch the pig. He did so, and not til morning did he find that he had helped to catch and load his own hog.

EX *Cabool Enterprise*, 8-24-1906

Prepare for Final Test

A farmer who never takes time to rest may come to his long vacation sooner than he expects.

Auxvasse Review, 3-27-1911

There will never be another crop of land. Better improve what you have.

St. James Progressive News, 12-26-1912

On most jobs men do not shirk,
but at gardening let women do the work.

Ashland Bugle, 5-26-1938

That's No Bull or Pork

An old farmer near Rolla undertook to hold a playful bull by the tail. His widow says Joseph was never known to stick to anything more than ten minutes at a time.

Cabool Enterprise, 5-29-1908

When you go to a first class hotel in the city and are charged 60 cents for a pork steak, don't get angry with the farmer. He probably only got about 8 cents for the pork. The difference in cost is for style.

Rolla Times, 4-7-1910

Ever Ask the Lad?

The father gives orders. He told his 12-year-old son to milk the cows, feed the horses, slop the pigs, hunt up the eggs, feed the calves, catch the colt and put him in the stable, cut some wood, split the kindling, stir the cream, pump fresh water in the creamery after supper, and to be sure he studied his lessons before he went to bed. Then he went to the farmers' club to discuss the question, "How to Keep the Boys on the Farm."

Clyde Times, 6-10-1910

And Bye, Bye to Sleep

No one who has not tried them, knows the value of husk beds. Certainly mattresses would not be used if husk beds were tried. They are not only more pliable than mattresses, but they are more durable. The first cost is but trifling. To have husks nice, they must be split—after the manner of splitting straw for braiding. The finer they are split, the softer will be the bed, although they will not be likely to last as long as when they are put in whole. Three barrels full, well-stowed in, will fill a good sized tick, that is, after they have been split. The bed will always be light, the husks do not become matted down like feathers and they are certainly more healthy to sleep on. . . . It is calculated that a husk bed will last from twenty-five to thirty years. Every farmer's daughter can supply herself with beds (against the time of need) at a trifling expense, which is quite an inducement now-a-days.

Clyde Times, 6-10-1910

Hadn't You Noticed Fashions?

"Women should wear what they like," says a famous sociologist. They usually do, dear, they usually do.

Tarkio Avalanche, 11-20-1908

The man who travels a thousand miles in a thousand hours may be tolerably quick footed, but he isn't a touch to the woman who keeps up with the fashions.

Trenton Western Pioneer, 8-30-1851

What You See Is What You Get

We read in an exchange an inquiry from a young lady as to the proper depth to cut the V-shaped waist. That's easy, let the limit be the waist band.

Salem Post, 1-10-1918

The split skirt is undoubtedly a fulfillment of scripture which says "those things which are hidden shall be made plain."

Smithville Democrat-Herald, 1-19-1914

Beauty may be skin deep, but it counts for a whole lot.
Wayland Hustler, 6-18-1908

Mary had a little frock, the latest style no doubt.
But when she got inside it, she was over half way out.
Ashland Bugle, 9-6-1917

It is no worse to put the big berries on top of the package to make it attractive than to dress a depraved human carcass in broadcloth for a similar purpose.
Eldon Advertiser, 5-16-1895

What Sparks a Shock Today?

Remember when sight of a stocking was ever so shocking?
Ashland Bugle, 7-22-1939

New bathing suits seem designed to be worn while taking a bath.
Jefferson City Capital News, 2-10-1922

In looking over the girls' dresses today it makes us revise the old adage and remark: "As ye show, so shall we peep."
Sikeston Standard, 4-19-1921

How Would Playboy Picture It?

We were in the store of one of our dressmakers yesterday and saw a most ingenious device invented for the purpose of enabling the ladies to delude our unsuspecting males by a "deceitful show," which is termed a "palpitator." It is an artificial bosom, made from a steel frame, which encloses a bellows, operated by clock work. The machinery gives that portion of the bosom which is intended to be looked upon, a gentle heaving motion about twenty times a minute. The effect is said to be wonderful. The palpitator may be readily attached to that garment worn to give shape to the body, which it gives support by aid of drilling, whalebone, eyelets, lacing &c.
St. Joseph Morning Herald, 6-28-1866

So That's the Reason

A woman's life (by rights) ought to be longer than a man's—it takes her so long to dress.

Richmond Missourian, 1-16-1919

Pleasant Weather Forecast

This witty remark was made by a young lady in St. Louis: "It is wisely ordained that the same wind that sweeps our dresses aside, also fills the eyes of naughty young men with dust."

Huntsville Herald, 2-8-1871

Life and Living Complicated

Use the bitter elements of life as medicine and feed on the sunshine.

Hartsburg Truth, 10-11-1907

Guidelines for Life

It is better to reform than to pose as a reformer.

Ashland Bugle, 9-6-1906

To see the bright side of life, use a little polish on yourself.

Ashland Bugle, 8-21-1939

The proper way to live is to try to improve on what is, instead of lamenting about what might have been.

Rock Port Atchison County Mail, 10-16-1896

Something for All

The grand essentials to happiness in this life are something to do, something to love, and something to hope for.

Eldon Advertiser, 1-17-1895

Profit by the mistakes your neighbor makes.

Ashland Bugle, 8-10-1920

Control Temper, Too

Don't raise your voice and your temper will never get very high.
Hartsburg Truth, 1-14-1921

Good temper wears better than a pretty face.
Lilbourn Herald, 5-22-1914

It is not necessary to lose your temper to prove that you have one.
Wayland Hustler, 6-18-1908

Death and Humor

After all, the world is a dangerous place—very few get out alive.
Pleasant Hill Local, 12-16-1886

New ways of prolonging life are discovered and announced almost every day, but Death hasn't found it out yet.
McFall Mirror, 1-9-1903

Positively a Cure

The only place where blame can rest easy is in a cemetery.
Shelbyville Shelby County Herald, 1-3-1900

Most men have to die to have decent things said about them.
Cabool Enterprise, 1-3-1900

Always on the Prowl

"If it wasn't for hope the heart would break," as the old woman said when she buried her seventh husband, and gazed anxiously among the funeral crowd for another.
Unionville Republican, 10-31-1867

Like Some Presidents?

Here's the real proof of a great man. Forty or fifty years after he is dead they began to print a lot of stories about him, setting forth interesting events in his career that never happened.
Lamar Democrat, 1-11-1909

No Air-Conditioning, Either

"When I die," said a married man, "I want to go where there is no snow to shovel." His wife said she presumed he would.
Memphis Conservative, 1-24-1878

If Nothing Else, Divorce

An Ohio Woman wants a divorce because her husband talks in his sleep. Perhaps it was the only chance he had.
Lamar Democrat, 5-29-1902

A pretty divorcee never lacks male defenders and apologists, no matter how bad she may be.
Parkville Platte County Gazette, 7-13-1899

Divorce is a blessing when love is stone dead.
Richmond Missourian, 4-10-1919

No Lesson Learned?

One of the strangest features about a divorce lies in the fact that few people want one until they get anxious to marry again.

Lamar Democrat, 5-29-1902

Very rarely does a man or a woman want a divorce until he or she also wants to get married again. The divorce is not the breaker of homes, for the homes are already broken up before it is applied for; it is actually the promoter of matrimony. Sounds funny, but it's true.

Lamar Democrat, 1-7-1909

Would Lawyers Concur?

The proposal to sell a marriage license with a divorce codicil is in the direction of thrift, drift and the spirit of the age. It is always advisable to buy a return-trip ticket.

Calhoun Clarion, 11-29-1902

That's All That's Wrong?

We were glancing over the Jasper county court records today when we noticed that a woman wanted a divorce for this: Her husband "was a habitual drunkard, was quarrelsome in disposition and often cursed her without cause; that on occasions he swore at her on the public square in Carthage; that on two or three different times he slapped her, falsely accused her of being untrue to him, and that he was of shiftless habits and failed to support her, and finally left her." Some women expect so much of a man, anyway.

Lamar Democrat, 4-9-1908

Slippery Legal and Political Issues

Editors of the past century were not as fearful about what they published in their newspapers as some journalists appear to be today. For one reason there weren't as many lawyers in those years who were waiting to charge some publication with libel.

The political front of the burgeoning nation and world was another favorite target for the newsmen. Many of their comments directed toward the federal and state governments frequently had some legal association.

Regardless of the subject, the editors used their pens frequently as they shared their personal and political views with their readers, often resorting to a humorous approach. Remember, editors and readers were well known to each other in those years.

Now and then, some editors even voiced optimistic views toward the prospects for women in politics. For the most part, women had not gained the right to vote when these editors were writing their messages for their subscribers.

Appropriate Today, Too

"Sir," said an old judge to a young lawyer, "you would do well to pluck some of the feathers from the wings of your imagination and stick them in the tail of your judgment."

Sedalia Bazoo, 7-16-1875

Doubtless many a married man will clip out and take home a Chicago judge's ruling that a wife has no right to warm her cold feet on her husband's back.

Trenton Weekly Times, 1-20-1910

If a client gets five thousand dollars his lawyer usually takes half of it, says the *Boonville Republican*, but if the client gets five years his attorney lets him have it all.

Ashland Bugle, 4-20-1922

But Not PC Today

A Chicago man insisted on keeping his hat on in the theatre because a lady in front of him kept hers on. The man was arrested and the lady—well, she still enjoys unequal rights.

Rock Port Atchison County Mail, 9-18-1896

A Philadelphia judge has decided that a husband is not bound to support a wife who smokes cigarettes.

Unionville Pantagraph, 2-12-1901

Unanswered Questions

'Tis said that Justice knows no law. Then why do we have so many lawyers?

Cabool Enterprise, 8-31-1906

A good lawyer is not a necessity for necessity knows no law.

Oregon Holt County Press, 11-23-1876

Careful What You Say

A Craig man went to a lawyer for advice. After receiving the retaining fee the lawyer said: "State your case." "Well, sir," said the client, "a man told me to go to h— and I want your advice." The attorney took down a volume of the Missouri statutes and after turning over a few leaves, answered: "Don't do it. The law doesn't compel you."

Oregon County Paper, 4-21-1882

An Ohio Man who left a will containing sixteen words, with no loopholes for a contest, must have made the lawyers up there very indignant.

Auxvasse Review, 12-22-1910

An effective libel law is doubtless essential but it prevents the public from learning the inside facts of many a political deal, and paves the way for the wholesome defrauding of the government.

Hallsville Eagle, 6-12-1903

Still, Life Goes On

A celebrated lawyer once said that the three most trouble-some clients he ever had were a young lady who wanted to be married, a married woman who wanted a divorce, and an old maid who didn't know what she wanted.

Clinton Advocate, 1-29-1885

The object of a blue law, it is said, is to keep men from painting the town red.

Ashland Bugle, 4-14-1938

A Justice of the Peace in marrying his first couple got the ceremony slightly mixed. He wound up by saying "Suffer little children to come unto them."

Paris Mercury, 9-30-1875

The great need in the criminal laws today is that they be so changed that society may get just a little of the protection which the accused so fully enjoyed.

Harrisonville Cass County Leader, 5-10-1906

And We'll Agree

In the circuit court I heard this dialog between opposing lawyers. One lawyer asked the other if he would admit certain things in the case. The other replied: "I admit nothing. I never admit anything. I do not admit that I am here in this courtroom right now." The opposing lawyer dryly remarked: "I will admit that you are not all here."

Albany Capital, 4-1-1934

The great function of law makers is to pass laws for the supreme courts to declare unconstitutional.

Sikeston Standard, 7-14-1916

How Would You React?

Almost every paper we pick up gives an account of outrages on women and girls by some devil in human shape, and in most cases, the culprit either gets off with a light sentence or goes free. On account of the delays of the law, the fact that money will procure the best legal talent in the land, who generally manages to cheat justice, we give it as our deliberate opinion that the only way to protect the women from these leacherous devils is to hang them as soon as caught. We believe that it would be doing God and the country a service to hang all rapists.

Paris Monroe County Appeal, 8-7-1885

Politics: Ahead of Schedule?

A college professor predicts that women will rule the world fifty years hence (1956). The change will not be perceptible.

Queen City Transcript, 3-2-1906

It may take years to do it, but women's vote will clean house.

Ashland Bugle, 12-22-1920

A miserable specimen of a male man says that giving the ballot to a woman would not amount to much, for none of them would admit that they were old enough to vote until they were too old to take any interest in politics.

Huntsville North Missouri Herald, 1-19-1870

Respect for Legislature?

There will be no extra session of the Legislature and everybody is glad of it. The last session has not as yet passed from the memory of the people.

Huntsville Randolph Democrat, 1-12-1900

Jefferson City church-goers showed how able they were to grasp fitting opportunities when they set their week of prayer for the same time that the legislature opened.

Pierce City Democrat, 1-23-1903

Well, the Legislature has adjourned. Little was done. The only necessary thing to be done was to undo the mischief that had been done by former legislatures it is now universally admitted. Repeal about a hundred bad laws and keep the Legislature from meeting for ten years would be the best thing that could happen.

Oregon County Paper, 4-8-1881

Creditable—The Missouri Legislature recently adopted a resolution to have public printing done by convicts, but it was found to be of no consequence, as it was ascertained there was not a printer in the penitentiary.

Vienna Central Missourian, 4-24-1861

Analogy—Son—Father, why under Heaven did the Legislature make so many Justices this year for? Father—When the potatoes are small we always put more in the hill, you know.

St. Louis Missouri Argus, 11-27-1835

Little Did They Know

The battleship *Maine* is now in the harbor of Havana and the American residents there will feel better.

Piedmont Banner, 1-27-1898

Congress Still the Same

It is said that Congress is about to investigate the high cost of living. It will not have to go very far to find one of the causes.

Aurora Advertiser, 4-8-1910

Some newspapers defined Congress as "the consolidated gas company."

Ashland Bugle, 10-3-1918

We note with excruciating pain that Congress shows signs of retrenchment in every direction except wherein their own interests are at stake.

Marthasville Record, 1-22-1915

Congress is still pegging away and doing nothing but drawing their salaries regularly. When anything is done we will inform our readers.

Paris Monroe County Appeal, 2-9-1883

Seems like Congress could work its jaws
For fewer and better laws.

Ashland Bugle, 3-31-1938

Congress resumed work (?) Monday.

Glasgow Journal, 1-8-1885

What About Today?

A delegate from Alaska? What possible right has that $12,000,000 icicle to a delegate in Congress?

Liberty Tribune, 2-10-1882

Many a man's honesty has saved him from becoming a politician.

Hartsburg Truth, 8-14-1903

And Politics in General

We can't have an honest election race
Until we get an honest human race.

Ashland Bugle, 3-23-1939

We wonder if any women politicians have to learn to cuss, tell smutty jokes, chew tobacco and smoke before they are fully educated in the ways of a successful politician.

Sikeston Standard, 5-5-1919

Women who go into politics should make a deep study of the methods of the men politicians—then stay clear of them.

Lewistown Record, 5-13-1920

The average man expects too much of the government and too little of himself.

Ashland Bugle, 7-21-1921

We have never tried it, but it must be fine to be a statesman and have nothing to do but view with alarm.

Ashland Bugle, 2-16-1922

Too Much of a Good Thing

Three men were sitting in a cafe. One of them was reading a newspaper. Suddenly he pointed to an article, shook his head and exclaimed: "Tut, tut." The second man looked over his shoulder, frowned and exclaimed: "Tut, tut, tut!" The third one jumped up and exclaimed: "If you two fellows are going to talk politics, I'm going home."

Washington Missourian, 7-6-1939

Other Political Concerns

It was a Missouri man, of course, who thus silenced a third-party advocate: "While there were only two parties in the Garden of Eden everything went well and they were both happy. But no sooner did the third party crawl in then the devil was to pay."

Paris Monroe County Appeal, 1-15-1892

The majority vote is seldom wrong but it is not always right.

Aurora Advertiser, 3-5-1909

Politics is making others believe what you don't believe yourself.

Ashland Bugle, 8-31-1905

Money, Taxes and All That

Worrying about money and taxes is nothing new. Comments a century or so ago by country editors often are as relevant today as they were when originally written.

In the business world the emphasis then was on railroad travel, while today it is on air traffic. But the problems are similar. Back then, the nation worried about "millions" of dollars spent for this or that; today the worry concerns "billions" or "trillions." Complaints, however, remain the same.

The emphasis then, as today, urged an individual to save for his/her future. Still, for most of the editors who usually encountered financial problems of their own, there were concerns more meaningful than money. It didn't take much for one to appear to be "rich" in the eye of the average editor.

Since editors needed advertising revenue to survive, they frequently related the value of the use of such space in their publications, pointing out examples that businessmen could adapt to improve their own financial rewards.

Economics and Tax Problems

Earn money before you spend it.

Lexington Caucasion, 5-16-1919

So many new kinds of taxes have been invented that they tax the memory.

Thayer News, 10-11-1918

Only in the Dog World

A dog lying on the hearth rug with his nose to his tail is the emblem of economy. He makes both ends meet.

Lexington Missouri Register, 2-15-1866

And Cheaper, Too

We have heard of an economical man who always takes his meals in front of a mirror—he does this to double his dishes. If that isn't philosophy, we should like to know what is.

Rolla Express, 7-30-1860

Where Your Heart Is

Did you ever hear a man with an obese bank balance say that the love of money was the root of all evil?

Auxvasse Review, 4-2-1908

Some people brag about their town but they want the other fellow to back up their opinion by putting up the money.

Aurora Advertiser, 5-8-1908

Money never yet has brought as good a time as a small boy can have with a crooked stick, a fish line, and a baited hook.

Auxvasse Review, 4-8-1909

For Her Retirement?

We have always wondered what women do with the two cents saved by purchasing a two dollar article for $1.98.

Plattsburg Clinton County Democrat, 7-26-1907

Work vs. Women's Rights

An eight-hour-a-day man on going home the other evening for his supper found his wife sitting in her best clothes, on the front stoop, reading a volume of travels. "How is this?" he exclaimed. "Where's my supper?" "I don't know," replied his wife. "I began to get breakfast at 6 o'clock this morning, and my eight hours ended at 2 o'clock in the afternoon."

Maysville Western Register, 8-13-1868

Ahead of His Time

By the year 2000, says an exchange paper, it is very probable that manual labor will have utterly ceased under the sun, and the occupation of the adjective hard-fisted will have gone forever. They have now, in New Hampshire, a potato digging machine, which, drawn by horses down the rows, digs the potatoes, separates them from the dirt, and loads them up into the cart, while the farmer walks alongside, singing "Hail Columbia!" with his hands in his pockets.

Hannibal Tri-Weekly Messenger, 8-28-1852

Top Bargain of Life

The public will please remember that I will keep a full line of coffins and undertakers' goods at Ashley. Mr. C. C. Burks will have charge of my business there and I propose to sell goods so cheap that no competition can equal my prices. I will sell coffins so low that it will actually pay you to die in order to take advantage of the prices.

Bowling Green Times, 5-31-1888

It is unfortunate that the birthday of Washington, the man who could not tell a lie, has to be celebrated during the season when income returns are being made out.

Sikeston Standard, 2-28-1930

New Airlines Get It

This is the time of the year when the average person goes away for a "change and rest," and some one has facetiously remarked: "The railroads get the 'change' and the hotels get the 'rest.'"

Hardin News, 7-21-1902

All in the Interpretation

"Please send me a side-saddle for a young lady with a red blush seat" was an order which a Springfield harness firm received the other day.

Hartsville Wright County Progress, 8-25-1899

Now Ten Billions?

Some fellow advocates the idea that fortunes should be limited to ten million dollars in this country. Come to think of it, most of them are.

Linneus Bulletin, 1-21-1903

Guaranteed Too

The devil is the only creditor that gives his customers hell.

Revere Current, 5-19-1898

If you try to keep up with the Joneses you will get behind with your grocerman.

Willow Springs News, 6-13-1935

The most serious operation is having your pay cut.

Jefferson City Capital News, 2-7-1922

Merchants Happy as Well

Man also differs from woman in this respect: When a man shops, he spends money.

Shelbyville Shelby County Herald, 2-12-1919

Still a Good Philosophy

No man was ever accused of being crazy because he devoted all his time to attending to his own business.

Plattsburg Clinton County Democrat, 3-15-1907

The man who does as little as he can for his wages is usually the man who complains about the wage scale.

Auxvasse Review, 6-23-1910

Prepare for the Future

If you had as much money as you think you ought to have, a lot of others wouldn't have as much as they need.

Salem News, 1-11-1923

Every time a man picks up a little experience he drops a few dollars. Money making is like quick sand: the more you get into it, the deeper you get.

Auxvasse Review, 1-21-1909

The poorest man in the world is one who has nothing but money.

Unionville Republican, 10-31-1867

Save what you can of your income instead of spending it foolishly, and some day when other people are eating prunes you may be in a position to eat strawberries.

McFall Mirror, 1-9-1903

Money Has Its Place

It's this way: After robbing Peter to pay Paul a man usually forgets to settle with Paul.

Ashland Bugle, 6-22-1905

The value of money depends on the tastes of the man who spends it.

Auxvasse Review, 3-18-1909

Now it costs more to live, but we live more.

Ashland Bugle, 8-4-1938

The Devil You Say

Money is the root of all evil, and most of us are rooting for it like the devil.

Ashland Bugle, 9-21-1911

Check Bounced at Gate

Money loses its purchasing power at the boundary line between this world and the next. A prize was once offered for the best definition of money, and a bright-eyed boy brought forth this: "An article which may be used as a universal passport to every-where except Heaven, and as a universal provider of everything except happiness."

Kahoka Free Press, 1-8-1929

Money does not make the man, but in the hands of a real man it adds to his effectiveness in the world's workshop.

Ashland Bugle, 9-15-1910

Sometimes More Often

A Chicago banker asked a young lady of that city what kind of money she liked best. "Matrimony," she replied. "What interest does it bring?" asked the inquisitive banker. "If properly invested it will double the original stock every two years," she replied.

Oregon Holt County News, 11-13-1857

Rich and Their Problems

Seek not to be rich, but happy; riches lie in bags, but happiness lies in content, which wealth can never give.

St. Louis American, 12-19-1844

It is preferable always to be poor rather than to be rich and then become poor. The most helpless creature in all the earth is the bankrupt child of luxury.

Hamilton News-Graphic, 6-17-1890

The price tag never accompanies a real Christmas gift.

Auxvasse Review, 12-14-1908

Advertising a BIG Award?

LOST—At the Festus Drug Co. on last Wednesday night. A Penny. Finder please return to F. J. Pratte and receive award.

Festus Tri-City Independent, 6-20-1913

But Who Is That One?

The *Salisbury Press-Spectator* says even the man who believes in newspaper advertising will sometimes say, "No, it won't pay me to advertise that; it appeals to too small a class of people." And yet that same man if he loses a bunch of keys will rush an ad to the newspaper office although he knows that in the wide, wide world there is but one individual who can possibly be influenced by that advertisement.

Fayette Howard County Advertiser, 3-8-1906

Two Bits for a Pig?

Scene in a Newspaper Office—Advertiser—"I have a pig strayed away, what do you charge to put him in the paper?" "It will depend on the size and number of words we use." "Is it the size? Well, then, Jimmy Smith paid but a dollar to put his horse in, and surely a pig is not so big as a horse."

St. Joseph Weekly Herald, 4-17-1862

Chickens Can Teach Too

The business man should learn from the busy hen. How could the world know she had laid an egg if she didn't open her mouth and advertise the fact?

Lebanon Republican, 7-19-1895

Preachers Share the Limelight

Early readers of American newspapers had more religious news available for their weekly pursuit than today's readers. The preachers, always well known in the community, were the subject of numerous editorial comments. On occasions, they would be praised, with some favorable words from the editor. On other occasions, they might be the subject of jokes or humorous remarks . . . some involving the preachers' children.

The traditional public opinion of the pioneer editor was not one that would justify these men as qualified to offer criticisms concerning the ministry. Yet who knows, while reading these comments today, how serious the writers were? No doubt some of these views were offered to readers to spark some action on their part.

The church was generally the center for community life, the place where families could gather for enjoyment along with others of similar religious interests. And this was especially true for the children, as some items reveal.

Sermon a Bit Confused

An anecdote is related of a young preacher at a city church, who had for his text a verse from the parable of the ten virgins, and in the course of the sermon explained: "That in old times it was customary when the bridegroom and bride were coming, for ten virgins to go out and meet them, and escort them home—five of these virgins were male, five female."

Palmyra Spectator, 5-8-1863

The more fuss a man makes when he gets religion, the less likely it is to stick.

Lamar Democrat, 6-3-1909

Grace on a Speed Trip

Three little boys were disputing as to whose father said the shortest grace. First Boy—My father says, "Lord we thank Thee for these provisions." Second Boy—And mine says, "Father bless this food for us." Third Boy—"Ah, mine he's best of all, he shoves the plate to mamma and says, 'Darn ye, fill up.'"

Forest City Independent, 3-5-1879

The Rev. George Bull baptized forty persons by immersion in twenty-seven minutes in Savannah, and he is eighty years old, too. He is a "star" baptizer—in fact, he is a Great Dipper.

Fulton Callaway Gazette, 10-5-1877

Did He Pass the Plate?

A preacher who visited the pen and talked to the convicts on Sunday began his remarks with "My friends, I am glad to see so many of you here today."

Fulton Callaway Gazette, 3-1-1878

The sooner a preacher realizes that religion is life the sooner he can make life religious.

Ashland Bugle, 12-20-1917

Spelling Lesson No. I

The dictionary spells "good" with two o's, the Bible with one.

Ashland Bugle, 12-14-1922

What's Your Interpretation?

It is impossible to look at the sleepers in church without being reminded that Sunday is a day of rest.

Cape Girardeau Eagle, 6-21-1862

It might help to lower taxes all along the line if all church property was subject to taxation the same as you and I. Most of that property is built for show more than for worship.

Sikeston Standard, 1-7-1930

Actions Speak Louder

If certain people would devote one-tenth of the time they spend in howling prayers to actual Christian service in feeding and clothing the poor and needy they would stand a better chance of getting to the heaven for which they yearn.

Aurora Advertiser, 10-29-1909

If, as some people aver, sin is the cause of this drought this summer we don't look for rain for a long time. There is plenty of sin in this old world to drive away moisture for a thousand years to come.

Queen City Leader, 7-25-1901

The beauty of the body is for a day; and the beauty of the soul is for eternity.

Memphis Conservative, 10-4-1877

Why is it easier to be a clergyman than a physician? Because it is easier to preach than to practice.

Oregon Holt County News, 9-25-1857

Look in the Mirror

There are plenty of boys in town who still have no inkling that they are made in the image of God.

Belton Herald, 10-25-1895

It is not the man who talks most about his religion that favorably impresses others, but the man who lives his religion. The man who is constantly saying what a good man he is and how he enjoys his religion is a man who, as a rule, will bear watching.

Sikeston Standard, 4-24-1914

About the only claim to piety some people have is a pious look.

Salisbury Democrat, 12-24-1909

Those who most readily find God to swear by seldom find him to pray to.

Savannah North-East Democrat, 9-13-1856

Obviously a Navy Man

A clergyman who married four couples in one hour remarked to a friend that it was "pretty fast work." "Not very," responded his friend, "only four knots an hour."

Sedalia Earth, 4-3-1886

Advice for Ministers

A preacher took for his text, "Feed My Lambs." A plain farmer very quaintly remarked to him on coming out of the church: "A very good text, sir, but you should take care not to put the hay so high in the rack that the lambs can't reach it."

Salisbury Bulletin, 3-11-1869

Sermonettes: Hope is the mother of disappointment. Heaven is gained by effort, not alone by results. Real sacrifice entails inconvenience. The preacher who is popular with everybody is missing some golden opportunities. "Bad luck" gets the blame for a lot of laziness.

St. Joseph Eye, 12-31-1909

"The poor shall be with us always." All right, then let's keep a few for samples instead of carrying millions in stock.

St. Louis Progressive Press, 2-20-1931

There is perhaps no place where people show their determination to trot along in the same old rut so much as in the church. And it's rather hard to tell whether it's the fault of the people or the church.

Aurora Advertiser, 9-10-1909

Pay Your Debts

If a man wills you a farm, it is his duty to die without delay; for what right has he, as a Christian, to delay you from the promised land?

Lexington Caucasion, 4-25-1866

There are people who are blessed with the beautific vision here on earth. They see the only God they worship every time they pass a mirror.

Calhoun Clarion, 11-8-1902

There isn't much difference in dressed chickens—human and fowl.

Jefferson City Capital News, 1-10-1922

A Sure Thing

"Life is so serious," says a Kansas City preacher, "none of us will get out of it alive."

Ashland Bugle, 2-18-1938

Man and/or Monkey?

We sorter believe with Bryan that man did not spring from the monkey. We also believe with the man who said if we did spring from the monkey we didn't spring far enough.

Ashland Bugle, 8-11-1921

Tell It in Verse

Now I wake me up to work,
I pray the Lord I may not shirk.

Ashland Bugle, 2-18-1938

The test of any religion now in use,
Is the kind of citizen it can produce.

Ashland Bugle, 2-27-1938

More Fish Stories Followed

The original truthful fish story is from the Bible: "And they toiled all night and caught nothing."

Ashland Bugle, 5-9-1912

Thankful in Thought

It is a boy's opinion that when the preacher offers thanks at the table he has a perfect right to peep to see if there is anything on the table worth giving thanks for.

Auxvasse Review, 11-5-1908

A gentleman, whose custom it was to entertain very often a circle of friends, observed that one of them was in the habit of eating something before grace was asked and determined to cure him. Upon the repetition of the offense he said: "For what we are about to receive, and for what James Taylor has already received, the Lord make us truly thankful."

Boonville Weekly Eagle, 1-27-1871

Long sermons are spoken of as clerical error.

Jefferson City Daily Eclipse, 11-8-1879

We realize there are stones in sermons when we get hit.

Auxvasse Review, 8-20-1908

Check the Birth Certificate

A small boy was prepared for Sunday School for the first time. His mother said the teacher would ask him who made him and he must answer "God." And, sure enough, the first thing the teacher asked him was "Johnnie, who made you?" The little chap hesitated a moment and then said: "I have forgotten the gentleman's name, but wasn't papa."

LaPlata Home Press, 5-19-1898

Some Seek the Easy Way

If a man's wife belongs to the church, he usually figures that she'll get salvation enough for the entire family.

Lamar Democrat, 6-10-1909

Perhaps if the Ten Commandments can be shortened sufficiently, they will be more easily remembered.

Marthasville Record, 4-9-1915

Limit the Talk, Preacher

There is a limit to all things. This old saying applies to sermons as well as anything else. When the preacher talks past 12 o'clock noon or 9 o'clock in the evening the average layman listener becomes restless and all the good of the forepart of the sermon is wasted.

Paris Monroe County Appeal, 6-29-1917

A preacher in Rolla has left the pulpit and in the future will act as agent for a life insurance company. The occupations are similar, one tries to teach a person how to live and the other insures one against death.

Fulton Sun, 1-16-1894

Now on Computers?

A new game has been introduced among social circles and it is likely to become popular. The amusement is called "Christianity." The girls all get on one side of the room and are the Christians, and the boys get on the other side and are heathens. Then the heathens all go over and embrace Christianity.

Potosi Journal, 8-19-1903

Hugging parties are the latest invention by charitable institutions and church societies. The hugs are sold as follows: Girls under 15 years 25 cents; from 15 to 20 years 50 cents; from 20 to 25 years 75 cents; another man's wife, $1; widows according to looks, 10 cents to $2; old maids 3 cents or two for a nickel.

Glenwood Criterion, 4-19-1883

Try the Balcony

If you are in the habit of going to sleep in church, you do not help the preacher any by occupying a front seat.

Rocheport Commercial, 1-10-1896

Heaven in the News

The road to Heaven and the road to wealth are two separate highways notwithstanding the efforts of a great many to combine them.

Hallsville Eagle, 5-30-1903

The average woman's notion of Heaven is to have a nice little bunch of money to go out and spend just exactly as she wants to, without anybody to butt in.

Lamar Democrat, 6-3-1909

A man died, says a Hume real estate agent, and the first day in Heaven he wanted to go sight-seeing, so the angel guide was given him. He noticed several persons with a ball and chain. "How is that," he asked the angel, "isn't this Heaven?" The angel smiled and said, "Yes, but these are not bad men; they come from Missouri and we have to chain them or they would go back."

Hume Border Telephone, 2-25-1910

Popular Missouri Authors?

"Who wrote the book of James?" asked a Sunday School teacher in an Iowa village. An innocent little fellow at the front of the class shouted, "The James boys."

Jefferson City Capital News Tribune, 1-27-1882

Pay Home Debts First

A North Missouri minister announced to his congregation recently that he wanted no member of his church to give to the foreign missionary cause, who owed the butcher, baker, grocer or printer. "Pay your local debts first," he said, "and then pay the debt you owe to the heathen." Report has it that the missionary collection was small but the respect of the congregation for the preacher was great.

EX *Cabool Enterprise*, 5-11-1906

Really a Family Performance

A certain preacher was holding forth to a somewhat wearied congregation when he "lifted up his eyes" to the gallery and beheld a youngster pelting the people below with chestnuts. Dominie was about to administer ex cathedra, a sharp and stringent reprimand for the flagrant act of impiety and disrespect, but the youth, anticipating him, bawled out at the top of his voice: "You mind your preaching, daddy, and I'll keep 'em awake."

Canton North-East Reporter, 11-10-1853

Doctors Have Their Problems

With a limited supply of doctors in the smaller communities as well as fewer medical facilities in these early years, it was only natural that many individuals turned to their weekly newspapers for advice on how to cure their ailments.

In addition, frequently so-called backwoods prescriptions were mentioned by the editors, who weren't adverse to poking fun at some doctors and their activities.

All too often, these problems continued to exist, as one editor wrote: "Some people suffer more from imaginary troubles than real ones." Today, the television world continues to "create" such "imaginary" illnesses.

Articles pointed out the danger from smoking and from drinking whiskey, although, unfortunately, many of those editors writing such material might have been smoking and/or drinking at the same time they were advising their readers on a better life.

Aside from advice from editors, cures were prominently displayed throughout the paper, as well. There were advertisements promising to remedy every ailment. For example, cures for baldness were plentiful. And they were probably as effective then as they are today.

Medical World Described

Pain is the price of all deep pleasure.
Lathrop Monitor-Herald, 12-6-1906

Never-heard-of-germs fill the air,
But people keep on living everywhere.
Ashland Bugle, 5-18-1939

A Russian scientist has traced all of a man's diseases to the fact that he wears clothes.
Platte City Landmark, 1-26-1894

The doctors have discovered that high-heeled shoes cause blindness. It has been noticed that a high instep and neatly turned ankle are also very straining on the eyes on windy days.

Princeton Peoples Press, 6-13-1894

Women are the chief patrons of the doctors, and they live longer than men. Does this seem one in favor of the M.D.'s or does it prove it's the people who are always ill that never die?

Lamar Democrat, 6-10-1909

Bargain Day (?) at the Doctor's

A doctor uptown gave the following prescription for a very sick lady a few days since: "A new bonnet, a new cashmere shawl, and a pair of gaiter boots!" The lady recovered immediately.

Oregon Holt County News, 8-21-1857

The trouble with the man who goes to see a doctor is that he wishes to be cured in a day of ills it has taken him years to acquire.

Doniphan Prospect-News, 1-25-1912

A young physician asked permission of a lady to kiss her. She replied: "No, sir, I never like to have a doctor's bill thrust in my face."

Paris Mercury, 6-10-1848

Texas invalids are appraised of their approaching decease by seeing the doctor trying on their coats and boots.

Platte City Landmark, 8-4-1871

No Refund Either

"I don't believe it is any use to vaccinate for small-pox," said a backwoods Kentuckian, "for I had a child vaccinated, and he fell out of a window and was killed in less than a week afterwards."

Liberty Tribune, 1-13-1882

Take That Nose Outside, Please

"How dreadful that cigar smells!" exclaimed Dobbs to a companion. "Why it's an awful smelling thing!"

"No, it's not the cigar that smells," was the reply. "What is it, then?" inquired Dobbs. "Why it is your nose that smells, of course, that's what noses are made for."

St. Louis Sentinel, 6-16-1855

Doctors Blame and Blamed

China is a remarkable country. The mother of the emperor was recently taken sick and was attended by 423 doctors, yet she recovered.

Fulton Sun, 12-29-1893

An exchange gives an illustration as follows: A doctor bet a man a dollar he could not get a billiard ball into his mouth. The man won the bet, but the doctor got fifteen dollars to get it out. Another form of advertising with the results about the same as usual, the advertiser spent one dollar and gets fifteen in return.

Lilbourn Herald, 1-30-1914

A medical student asked a famous surgeon: "What did you operate on that man for?" "Two hundred dollars," replied the surgeon. "Yes, I know that," said the student. "I mean what did the man have?" "Two hundred dollars," replied the surgeon.

Auxvasse Review, 1-13-1910

Some Such Folks Still Around

Some people suffer more from imaginary troubles than real ones. They always worry about the future and conjure up difficulties that do not exist. Because of this their life is robbed of more than half its joy and blessings.

Martinsburg Audrain County Oracle, 1-6-1910

Probably Guaranteed Too

An observing individual in a very healthy village, seeing the sexton at work in a hole in the ground, inquired what he was about. "Digging a grave, sir." "Digging a grave? Why I thought people didn't die often here—do they?" "O, no, sir, they never die but once."

Albany Ledger, 12-31-1868

Just Can't Win

When I was young I was poor; when old I became rich, but in each condition I found disappointment. When the faculties of enjoying were bright, I had not the means; when the means came, the faculties were gone.

Columbia Missouri Sentinel, 4-8-1852

First the Vote, Then . . .

Women are living longer then they did twenty-five years ago, but the doctors aren't agreed on the reason. Though all admit it isn't due to the spread of the suffrage movement, they are widely divided in their opinions. Statistics compiled in England show that the expectation of life of a woman of fifty is a year greater than it was in 1875 while that of a man is only a few months greater. One school of doctors, who believe that death is due entirely to a wearing out of brain tissues, says the longevity of women is due to the fact that they don't use their brains as much as men. On the other side of the scientific fence is a group of doctors who insist that woman lives longer now because she is more sheltered . . . doesn't have to face the wearing competition of business . . . and spends most of her time at home which is more airy and healthful than the offices where men work.

Clinton Daily Republican, 3-31-1913

But Still That Taste!

An old physician of the last generation was noted for his brusque manners and old-fashioned methods. One time a lady called on him to treat her baby who was lightly ailing. The doctor prescribed castor oil. "But doctor," protested the young mother, "castor oil is such an old-fashioned remedy." "Madam," replied the doctor, "babies are old-fashioned things."

Linn Unterrified Democrat, 1-16-1908

Unless They Watch TV?

Men seldom die or get mad during the first two hours after dinner.

Richmond Missourian, 9-5-1901

It is said that worry kills more people than work—probably because more people worry than work.

Richland Mirror, 1-11-1923

Baldness, an Ancient Cure

A loafer says that the best remedy for baldness is to rub whiskey on your head until the hairs grow out, "then take inwardly to clinch the roots."

Lexington Missouri Register, 5-28-1865

Old-Timers Remember

While a kid nearly a hundred years ago, mothers would put five drops of turpentine on a lump of sugar to give to each of the children. This was a practice in all well-regulated families and was given for worms. We hesitate to recommend this dose to some flappers we have seen who wiggle a great deal, but it might prove a blessing and be a permanent cure.

Sikeston Standard, 1-17-1930

Colds Always a Challenge

Of all other means of curing colds, fasting is the most effectual. Let whoever has a cold eat nothing whatever for two days, and his cold will be gone, provided he is not confined to his bed, because by taking that surplus which caused his disease to breath, he soon carries off the disease by removing the cause. This will be found more effectual if he adds copious water drinking to protracted fasting. By the time a person has fasted one day and night he will experience a freedom from pain and a clearance of mind in delightful contrast to that mental stupor and physical pain caused by colds. And how infinitely better is this breaking of colds than medicines!

Columbia Missouri Sentinel, 1-25-1852

A hot lemonade is one of the best remedies for a cold. It acts promptly and efficiently, and has no unpleasant after affects. One lemon should be properly squeezed, cut in slices, put with sugar, and covered with half a pint of boiling water. Drink just before going to bed, and do not expose yourself the following day. This remedy will ward off any attack of chills and fever if used promptly. We give it on the recommendation of one of the judges of our courts who is a just man and never takes bribes.

Neosho Times, 12-26-1872

Smoking Techniques, Dangers

Do not smoke either while fasting or for a short time before meals.

Union Franklin County Tribune, 11-22-1901

Did you ever see good molars in the mouth of a man who chews tobacco to "preserve his teeth"?

Hartsburg Truth, 8-14-1903

There's always hope for the man who is ashamed that he chews tobacco.

Platte City Argus, 11-28-1901

Convenient—A loving couple "down east" have had a pipe made with two handles, so that they can both smoke at the same time.

St. Louis American, 12-12-1844

When Start, When Stop Smoking?

A Kansas City centenarian says that he did not take up smoking until he was 96. He wisely avoided the chance of acquiring a bad habit until he had reached the age of discretion.

King City Chronicle, 3-20-1908

Lots of men with ordinary will power have quit smoking. But even a Puritan can't help sending a frazzled collar to the laundry just for one more time.

Warrenton Banner, 2-2-1917

When the gods love a man and want him in a hurry, they first make him smoke anywhere from twelve to thirty cigarettes a day.

Cassville Republican, 2-13-1902

Still a Debate?

A lady wants to know why the railroad companies do not provide special cars for tobacco chewers as well as for smokers. Bless her innocent heart, tobacco chewers are not so particular as that. An ordinary passenger car is good enough for them.

Kansas City Star, 11-4-1880

Century Ahead of Schedule

A society for the prevention of cigarette smoking will be organized tonight at the Centenary M. E. Church, St. Louis. Similar societies should be organized in every city, town, village and hamlet in the country. This pernicious habit is undermining the constitution and retarding the brain development of the youth of this country. Success to the undertaking.

St. Charles Monitor, 10-11-1894

What's Your Whiskey Order?

Some people borrow trouble, others buy it by the glass or bottle.

Plattsburg Clinton County Democrat, 4-26-1907

It will not pay to license saloons in Columbia. It will be a bad investment every way. Criminal costs will be increased, the burden of taxation made greater and the interests of the University injured.

Columbia Missouri Herald, 7-7-1892

Certainly a "Sure Cure"

A Chicago man said he couldn't stop drinking and then proved that he could by committing suicide. Some men are so contradictory.

Jamesport Gazette, 9-19-1905

The man who tries to drown trouble in alcohol usually gets out of depth and drowns himself.

Sikeston Standard, 11-5-1915

A report comes from Colorado that a Yale chemist has succeeded in fastening a rattlesnake's head to an adder's tail and make one snake out of two. The brand of whisky he used is not mentioned.

Lamar Republican, 8-22-1901

Some Drinking Guidelines

A few glasses of rye causes one to feel his oats.

Ashland Bugle, 4-11-1907

Old age always has been and always will be respected— more so than ever now, provided it has been bottled for two years or more.

Ashland Bugle, 11-24-1921

It has been wisely said that one difference between a bootlegger and a rattlesnake is that the bootlegger sells his poison.

Kahoka Free Press, 1-29-1929

Some females have been arrested in Kentucky for the manufacture of illicit whiskey. EX. That must be a mistake. No woman could ever have been arrested for keeping still.

Sedalia Bazoo, 10-4-1881

How's the Fat Content?

It is said that beer makes the blood vessels brittle, whiskey eats out the stomach and ruins the nerves, while tobacco stops the heart. What's the use for a fellow to live, anyway?

Lamar Democrat, 6-2-1902

Carrie Nation Egged

Carrie Nation objected seriously to the ovation of eggs she received in London, but she may draw the consoling thought from the episode that the eggs that were used for target practice on her can never, never be mixed in cheering draughts of eggnog on Tom and Jerry.

Harrisonville Democrat, 2-11-1909

Who Gains? Who Loses?

The *Sturgeon Leader* says they have four saloons in that village and that they are doing good business. This may be so, but we'll bet a cent that their customers are not doing very well, or at least their families are not in as good fix as the saloon keepers. Did you ever think about what darned fool the average dram drinker is? He spends two or three dollars a week at a saloon, the saloon man and his family dress well and ride in a carriage, while the poor devils who keep them up wear old clothes, live on sow-belly, and walk, if they go at all. If this picture ain't true, we hope to go to heaven in a week.

Paris Monroe County Appeal, 9-9-1881

Animals Always Attention Getters

Journalists have always recognized the importance of animals in feature stories. The public loves to read about animals and their activities, especially when they are involved with children.

Creatures were often kept for practical purposes. The chickens, for example, played a major role on many a farm. And much interest was displayed about their eggs—a source for outside money for the farmer's wife, and a source of meat for the family.

Animal stories were used to preach lessons as well, offering accounts that children could comprehend. Animals on the farms played a more significant role then than they do today. Especially the mule, who received extensive coverage in the press. Still, the bee, the cow, even snakes captured the editors' attention.

First, the Busy Ant

An exchange tells this one: An ant was grazing longingly at the carcass of a dead horse and a bootlegger's car passed and a jug of liquor bounced off the car and broke. The ant took one drink of the stuff and then grabbed the dead horse by the tail and shouted, "Come on, big boy, we're going home."

Wyconda Reporter-Leader, 4-2-1931

The Bee and Boys

The sting of a bee is only one thirty-second of an inch long, yet the average boy has no difficulty in finding it when he stirs up a hive.

Appleton City Journal, 9-21-1882

Cats Share Glory

Jones is a precise man. He has a cat sired by an old time back-fence yowler, while the mater is a Maltese tabby. He wishes to know if the offspring can be properly called a "Maltese cross."

Hamilton News-Graphic, 9-25-1884

The cat is a very modest beast, but, like so many sweet girls, it thinks that it can sing.

Richmond Missourian, 1-23-1902

Chickens High in the News

If a hen has a right to cackle, a rooster has a right to crow.

Ashland Bugle, 12-1-1938

A St. Louis judge has ruled that a chicken is not a nuisance. It certainly isn't, provided it is well done.

EX *Sedalia Daily Capital*, 1-5-1911

By actual count it has been proved that there are 8,120 feathers on a chicken. If you don't believe it, just count them.

Carl Junction Evening Graphic, 1-5-1907

Sex of eggs: Science and experience have sufficiently demonstrated that everything that bears must possess both the male and female qualifications, but perhaps it is not generally known that such is the case with eggs. I have found the following rule: I raise as many pullets among my chickens as I wish to, while some of my neighbors complain that their chickens are nearly all roosters and they cannot see why there should be any difference. I will tell you here what I told them, and for the benefit of those who do not know, that the round small eggs are the female ones, and the long slender ones are males. This rule holds good among all birds. So if you wish to raise pullets set the small round eggs; if you wish to raise roosters set the long slender ones. In this way you will be able to raise whichever sex you wish to.

Glenwood Criterion, 4-12-1883

New Killing Method

An exchange says: The old-fashioned way of killing chickens by wringing their heads off belongs to the dark ages. The only up-to-date way is to hang the chicken up by the feet and cut its head off. To this way the blood runs out leaving the meat clean and white. Try it once and you will never wring another chicken's head off.

LaGrange Indicator, 1-19-1899

The fact that his pet bantum had very small eggs troubled little Johnny. At last he was seized with an inspiration thus: Johnny's father, upon going to the fowl run one morning, was surprised at seeing an ostrich egg tied to one of the beams, with this injunction chalked above it: "Keep your eye on this and do your best."

Union Star Pinhook News, 2-22-1912

No man on earth can love his neighbor as himself if he has a garden and the aforesaid neighbor keeps chickens.

Hartsburg Truth, 9-10-1915

Electrify the Cow

A Kansas man has just succeeded in getting a patent on an electric motor fashioned on a cow's back, the electricity being generated by a dynamo attached to her tail. It strains the milk and hangs up the pail and strainer. A small phonograph accompanies the outfit and yells "So!" when the cow moves. If she kicks a hinged arm catches the milk stool and lams her over the back.

Linn Unterrified Democrat, 1-24-1907

The evil that men do live after them. Cows likewise do not give oleomargarine until they are dead.

Rock Port Atchison County Mail, 7-29-1880

No, my dear Lysbeth, a cow does not give milk, but you can take it from her.

Richmond Missourian, 1-23-1902

Undercover Workers Select Cows

Vigilance Committee—We are reliably informed that a vigilance committee is to be organized by a number of cow owners of the north part of the city for the purpose of putting a stop to the prevailing habit of some petty thieves who have been milking cows that did not belong to them. They are said to catch the cows while grazing in the woods, north of town, and milk them in the middle of the afternoon. They are known to some and all they want to do is to catch them in their nefarious work, and then all bets are off with Mr. Thief.

Poplar Bluff Weekly Republican, 9-24-1903

Dogs Rate High

Some women pay more attention to their dogs than they do their husbands, but then maybe the dogs growl less.

Salem Dent County Post, 10-3-1912

A Sad Bereavement

Old "Watch Maxfield" is dead—he was a good old pup, entirely harmless and worthless. He departed this life on Tuesday last at his last residence on Summer Street. The cause of his untimely decease was a shortness of breath, which finally ceased altogether, and disdaining to live longer, under the circumstances, he died. He was a superior breed of dogs—part pointer, part setter and part bear. He would point a bone, and set down to eat it, and barely left any meat on it. He was perfectly friendly with hogs—would not touch one for the world although he was frequently instigated to such atrocious deeds by such remarks as "sick-em Watch" and the like. Watch was a rather corpulent dog and many a hungry butcher's eye has been opened wide in contemplation of the delightful sausages into which he might be converted.

Farewell old dorg, no more you'll howl,
And wake the neighbors far and near,
No more we'll tremble at your growl,
On your nocturnal visits fear.
Above your grave we'll raise a stone,
And on that stone record your death.
And in these simple words alone—
"This poor dorg died for want of breath."

Weston Border Times, 1-25-1867

"Jiggs" Well Known

"Jiggs," the old, underslung British bulldog who was a familiar figure around the *Tribune* for more than a year, died yesterday. "Jiggs" was old and almost toothless yet he never stopped fighting, and for this reason he was taken from the *Tribune* office and given to Paul Bell. Mr. Bell kept the old dog at his barn on Ash, and for several months had fed him nothing but milk and eggs. He was buried on the banks of Flat Branch.

Columbia Tribune, 8-10-1926

Forget Your Problems

Oh, yes, we know we have more faults than some dogs have fleas, but like the dog with fleas, our faults make us forget our other troubles.

Sikeston Standard, 8-23-1921

Ducks in Hot Water

A Yankee in Iowa has taught ducks to swim in hot water, and with such success that they lay boiled eggs. Who says this is not an age of improvement?

Ste. Genevieve Plaindealer, 1-29-1853

Time Helps Fishing

Some of the fish caught last summer are now six feet long.

Jefferson City Capital News, 2-19-1922

Deal of a Lifetime?

A Macon paper tells of an Iowa man who was looking for farm land in South Missouri and when the real estate man got him down in the timber he noticed mud marks on the trees which looked as though they might have been left there by a flood. He asked the real estate man what did it. "Hogs," replied the real estate man. "They wallow in the mud and then rub against the trees." As they proceeded the Iowa man noticed that the mud marks rose higher and higher on the trees until on some it was ten feet from the ground. When they got back to town the real estate man asked him if he would like to buy some of the land. "I don't believe I want any of your land," replied the Iowa man, "but, say, I would like to buy a carload of your hogs."

Sarcoxie Record, 4-3-1904

The town council of Shelbina, Shelby county, has enacted an ordinance prohibiting all swine "ranging under forty pounds" from running at large on the streets. The world over, it is the practice to punish the little rogues and let the great ones go free.

St. Louis Republican, 7-19-1869

The difference between some men and a hog is that the hog knows when he had enough and the men don't.

Hallsville Eagle, 5-30-1903

Horses Have Their Place, Too

Behind the horse you see a lot of little country. In an automobile you see little of a lot of country.

Ashland Bugle, 6-17-1920

On Saturday last a horse belonging to Mr. Gill, of our town, was arrested for foraging from a farmer's wagon. It seems the farmer had just deposited a sack of flour in his wagon and stepped into an establishment to get some other articles, returning he found a loose horse had made sad havoc of his flour. Forth with making complaint to the Marshal, the animal was duly arrested. The owner, Mr. G., hearing of his horse's arrest, appeared on the premises and agreed to pay the damages, $2.00 for the flour and $1.00 for the arrest of said horse. This is not the first instance of this same horse foraging out of wagons from the county, but on several occasions has destroyed sundry articles that the country folks have left in their wagons. The farmers have just cause for complaint for these depredations, and there is not an ordinance to prevent animals from running at large in our streets. It is time there should be something done for the protection of our farmers when they have articles thus destroyed. There is also a cow that makes her living by foraging on the streets, and our country friends no doubt would rejoice to hear of her arrest and exile from the town.

Edina Sentinel, 2-24-1876

The man who is cruel to his horse is also not kind to his family. And the man who will kick a dog just because he is a dog, will slap and cuff his children around for no reason at all.

EX *Iberia Sentinel*, 1-23-1914

James Russell, a one-legged soldier, who recently stopped a runaway horse by pushing his wooden leg through the carriage wheel, stopped another dangerous runaway in New Hampshire last week. He has saved four lives and has been given a medal by the Humane Society.

Kansas City Times, 7-2-1881

Maybe Darwin Was Correct

After all, it is only fair to attempt to make a man of a monkey, since so many monkeys have been made of men.

Salem Dent County Post, 10-7-1912

Why Raise Mules?

Here are some of the very good reasons given by a well-known writer why farmers should raise more mules:

They can be raised cheaper than any other stock. They will go to the market much younger than any horse. They can be handled at two years old, and, if properly managed, will do as much work as a four-year-old horse and be better for it. They avoid danger and do not get into holes or dangerous places. If they run away they seldom hurt themselves or anything else much. They are less subject to disease than any other stock, and not liable to get blemished by wire or otherwise. I have raised mules a number of years and never had one blemished, but have had five horses nearly ruined. They stand heat much better than horses, if you do not think so, try a span on your binder some hot sultry day by the side of your horses. They can stand more abuse and hardship than the horse, but appreciate good treatment more than any other animal living, and live to a greater age than horses. There is profit in mule-raising because of quicker growth, being marketable at three years old. A horse has to be five years old. The writer nearly always has a good bunch of mules, and has not been kicked but twice in twenty years, and both times by a horse. I have sold a number of two-year-old mules for $150 each. EX *Fulton Sun.*

Columbia Missouri Herald, 1-6-1905

There is nothing more musical than the voice of one mule to another.
Shelbyville Shelby County Herald, 3-21-1900

Snakes Have Their Fun

The boa constrictor had got the half-grown chicken comfortably swallowed. He glanced complacently at the small rabbit that was sleeping in the opposite corner of the cage. "And now I will proceed to take down my hare."
EX *St. Joseph Times,* 9-14-1897

A snake got in bed with a young man at Hannibal the other night, and the young man got out.
Platte City Landmark, 6-23-1871

Snakes have frequently been known to commit suicide. Rattlesnakes, when surrounded by a circle of fire, will bite themselves to death.
Kahoka Clark County Courier, 1-26-1900

Spiders Offer Advice

The race is not always for the swift. The cussedness and cunning of the spider enables it to get away with the fly.
California Greenback Derrick, 3-25-1882

The spider is seldom in danger when his life is hanging by a thread.
Huntsville Randolph Democrat, 1-5-1900

Education a Major Concern

The Bible and newspapers were considered major educational tools by these early settlers. No doubt the majority of these newspaper readers developed their skills while on the job—farmer's sons were expected to follow farming, so they learned while doing the chores and other duties. Editors continued to warn readers of the dangers that would follow for those who failed to get a better education, on the farm or elsewhere.

Reading was a major concern, but there were also warnings about what one should read. When a person is better educated he will know more useful words and thus might stop cussing, editors advised.

Truth was stressed as well. And readers were alerted about the dangers that could come from too much emphasis on pride. And there was plenty of discussion about the definition of success—with greatly varying answers.

Editors also recommended that one could learn, too, from participation in civic affairs. Editors usually credited individuals when they performed worthwhile community service.

Still May Be True

"Pa, what's a symposium?" "It's sort of a meeting, my boy, so called because a lot of simps usually pose at 'em."
St. James Republican, 1-27-1916

Teach young men to rely upon their own efforts—to be frugal and industrious—and you have furnished them with a productive capital which no man can ever wrest from them.
St. Joseph Adventure, 5-15-1850

True Then, True Today

A Bible and newspaper in every house, a good school in every district—all studied and appreciated as they merit—are the principal support of virtues, morals and civil liberty.

St. Joseph Western News, 11-25-1881

Know Your ABCs

What vowel is the happiest? I, because it is always in bliss. What vowel is the most unhappy? E, because it is always in hell. What about the other vowels? They are in purgatory.

Shelbina Torchlight, 2-7-1890

But Not in the 1990s

Sex segregation is now in the air—not only is co-education becoming unpopular in the great colleges and universities, but even in the Government offices in Washington very few women are now appointed or desired.

Calhoun Clarion, 11-22-1902

Same Answer Today?

"What is your boy learning at college?" "I don't know. I can only tell you what he is studying."

Osceola St. Clair County Democrat, 4-13-1911

Conditions Go On and On

The American people are very prone to boast about the money they spend on education. Nothing could make a poorer boast. The amount looks big in the aggregate, but it is really trifling when analyzed. And the fact is that we pay our teachers a wage too small to be spoken of without a blush.

Lathrop Monitor-Herald, 11-29-1906

A fellow with only book learning is the most useless cuss on earth.

Cabool Enterprise, 8-31-1906

The public schools, at least in this section of the country, are not what they should be. This is due to many causes, chief of which is a failure on the part of parents to sustain the teacher . . . if a teacher is forced to punish a child . . . it will be found that the parent is against the teacher.

Lamar Democrat, 2-7-1901

A little boy, after watching the burning of the school-house until the novelty of the thing had ceased, started down the street saying, "I'm glad the old thing burned down; I didn't have my jogfry lesson, no how!"

Keytesville Herald, 8-10-1872

Remember Your First Year?

Many a bright college student has wished he knew as much as he thought he knew when he entered the freshman year.

St. Louis Argus, 1-22-1915

Watch Them Commas

The following sentence from a recently written novel strongly shows the importance of proper punctuation: "He entered on his head, his helmet on his feet, armed sandals upon his brow, there was a clod on his hand, his faithful sword in his eye, an angry glare he sat down."

Fredericktown Conservative, 6-14-1862

Still Some Around

A school master, who had an inveterate habit of talking to himself when alone, was asked what motive he could have in talking to himself. Jonathan replied that he had two good and substantial reasons: in the first place he liked to talk to a sensible man, and in the next place he liked to hear a man of sense talk.

Canton Missouri Plebian, 9-15-1848

Now Called "Communication"

SKOOL ROOLS—Not many miles from a town called Newburn, a lady is keeping school. She sent the following rules to the *Times*, provided by trustees for the government of the school: No swearin. No fitin. No quarrelin. No nicknamin. No goin into the water. No raslin and jumpin. No goin into any persons vine peaches or orchards without the consent of the owner. No pinchin. No stickin of pins in each other. No pullin of hair durin books. No courtin in skool. No writin of love letters in skool. Not more than one poopil must go out at a time, unless for wud and water. No crackin of walnuts, unless dried. No wishperin.

Mt. Vernon Spring River Fountain, 3-14-1867

Learn About Your State

A Missouri girl, Hattie Pomeroy, 22 years of age, who had been dragged from Appleton City, Mo., to Palisades, Colo., by her family, drank carbolic acid last week because she had rather die than live away from her old Missouri home. Nobody who has ever lived in Missouri can blame her.

Bethany Democrat, 10-20-1904

"A young woman," says the Ralls County Record, "who lives at Burlington, Kan., came to Missouri to commit suicide. This shows that a person would rather die in Missouri than live in Kansas."

Fulton Telegraph, 9-9-1898

Which Do You Prefer?

There is a discussion among Missouri newspapers of the proper pronunciation of the name of their state. It seems understood that the plain people call it "Mizzou-ree" and the patrician folk "Missou-rah" (a Philadelphia newspaper).

Columbia Missouri Statesman, 1-14-1892

Learn About Your Town, State

The man who continually knocks his hometown is generally the man who does the least for it and receives his all from it.

Ashland Bugle, 5-14-1917

Often as I have seen the aphorism "I'm from Missouri, you must show me," in print and heard it in conversation I never knew its origin or fully comprehended its significance until a few days ago. As it originated with a citizen of Boone county who died a few years ago, I became interested in its history, as follows: Never mind that it originated at a game of poker in Hot Springs, Ark., for such, I am informed by a party who was present, is the fact. An exciting and heavy game of poker was in progress, during which the players simply declared their hands and did not show them, for they were of the highest class of sportsmen and trusted each other. Of the party, however, was a Missourian who did not personally know those who either dealt or held the cards, and when it came to "call" (is this the proper word?) the rival players, he said with genuine Missouri emphasis, "You gentlemen are from Kentucky, Texas, Tennessee and Arkansas and seem to trust each other, but I'm from Missouri and you must show me," and they all did so. And thus originated the saying.

Columbia Missouri Statesman, 12-13-1901

Still More Pride in State

An Illinois exchange says a Missouri girl was hugged to death. That's a mistake, you can't kill them that way.

Huntsville Herald, 9-14-1871

Disagreement in World of Education

The legislature failed to appropriate money to the support of that great fraud, the Agricultural College at Columbia, and the Columbians are mad. This is the college with 10 professors and 12 students. Farming can only be learned by actually working on a farm.

Paris Monroe County Appeal, 4-3-1885

A University of Missouri professor says that few students can find brain space for an elective chain of thought.

Ashland Bugle, 12-5-1912

Epigram of Note

It was Walter Williams of the *Columbia Herald* (later President of the University of Missouri) who said: "Fame has taken men from the forge, the plow and the carpenter's bench, but she was never known to reach over a picket fence and snatch a dude out of a hammock." Honorable Champ Clark pronounces it the finest epigram uttered in America recently.

Ashland Bugle, 9-3-1903

Look at Our Presidents

Every American boy and girl should rejoice to live in the United States for there is no government limit to their laudable ambitions, and the very highest office in the land is open to the ambition of the poorest lad.

Rich Hill Western Enterprise, 7-18-1902

Learn Not to Cuss

When our editor can't get himself cussed occasionally he shows signs of declining mentality and advancing senility. Cuss away.

Smithville Democrat-Herold, 1-12-1917

A Habit or an Excuse?

The world is full of people who mistake abuse for ridicule and profanity for wit.

Hume Border Telephone, 9-26-1896

When in doubt, scratch your head, but don't cuss.

EX *Marshall Saline Citizen*, 9-23-1911

Promiscuous swearing is a jay habit. The loud mother-swearer, who likes to show how much he can "cuss" in public, is always a greenhorn. While some intelligent men use profanity occasionally, they are never proud of it and never use it to offend the ears of chance passersby. The habit is steadily declining among thoughtful people.

Linneus Bulletin, 2-4-1903

Learn the Truth, Too

Truth and daring is the price paid for progress.

Cole Camp Courier, 8-8-1901

Truth travels by stage coach—falsehood by telegraph.

Maysville Western Register, 8-20-1868

Somebody says truly that the first ingredient in conversation is truth, the next is good sense, the third good humor, and the last wit.

St. Louis American, 12-9-1844

Those who hold the truth in arrogance will find it slipping from their grasp.

Rich Hill Tribune, 8-15-1901

Whom Do You Trust?

Americans are a trustful people. Our coins have the motto, "In God We Trust." And during prohibition we trusted our bootlegger. We are all trying to trust our banker. Too many of us trust the stranger who offers a ten dollar check for a ten cent purchase. Many merchant has trusted until he was busted. We trust our cars to hold together at a mile-a-minute speed. We trust our politicians when they make promises during the campaign. But we don't believe everything we read in the newspapers, especially if it doesn't coincide with our desires.

Shelbina Democrat, 2-20-1935

Education Brings Success

Too many people measure a man's success by what he gains instead of by what he deserves.

Portland Ledger, 1-31-1901

The successful man is the man who lives most, whose interests in life are most vital, whose sympathies are broadest, whose charity is widest, who sees most, feels most, enjoys most.

Odessa Democrat, 12-8-1904

Whatever the world may say concerning the elements and conditions of success, it remains true that every life is a failure that does not grow better as it grows older.

Macon Times, 1-23-1891

Know When to Talk

Loud talking gives little except contempt for the talker.

Sturgeon Leader, 11-14-1901

Don't talk too much; it's dangerous, and besides you seldom learn anything while you are talking. Get the other fellow's idea; let him talk. It may even make him your friend.

Walnut Grove Tribune, 1-14-1904

Talk's cheap, but all good things began with talk. A street fair is a subject for such talk around Hartsburg now. Let's have it.

Hartsburg Truth, 4-19-1907

Better Understand Success

The way to success is simple. Think of the right thing to do. Think of it first. Do it. Do it first. And there you are.

Columbia Missouri Herald, 4-27-1900

Never depend on other men to help you achieve success. This is a cold, a selfish and unfriendly world, and he who does not fight his own battles is likely to fall by the wayside.

Hamilton News-Graphic, 1-31-1890

He who cannot dream cannot do.

Lathrop Monitor-Herald, 12-6-1906

The secret of happiness and success is constant work.

Lathrop Monitor-Herald, 5-23-1907

Many good things come to those who hustle while they wait.

Shelbyville Shelby County Herald, 2-19-1919

History: A Key to Education

Life a Century Ago (1801)
One hundred years ago a man could take a ride on a steamboat. He could not go from Washington to New York in a few hours. He had never seen an electric light or dreamed of an electric car. He could not send a telegram. He couldn't talk through the telephone. He never heard of the hello girl. He could not ride a bicycle. He had never received a typewritten communication. He had never heard of the germ or worried about bacili and bacteria. He never looked pleasant before a photographer or had his picture taken. He had never taken a ride in an elevator. He had never imagined such a thing as a typewriter. He had never used anything but a wooden plow. He had never seen his wife using a sewing machine. He had never struck a match on his pants or anywhere else. He couldn't take an anesthetic and have his leg cut off without feeling it. He had never purchased a 10-cent magazine which would have been regarded as a miracle of art. He had never seen a McCormick reaper or a self-binding harvester. He had never crossed an iron bridge. In short there were several things that he could not do and several things he did not know.

Joplin News-Herald, 1-4-1901

Feature Stories Attract Readers

Newspaper editors have always recognized their readers' special interest in feature stories off the beaten path about unusual persons or incidents.

Frequently such stories highlighted some event in the community. However, if the incident was so out of the ordinary, it hardly mattered where the event occurred. And as seen in earlier chapters, when children and animals are involved, the interest became greater and received better coverage.

Feature stories were commonly about a new interpretation or definition of a word or a phrase, an unusual approach to education, or an experiment the editor found worth reprinting.

Along with feature stories came numerous mentions of food. Hardly a newspaper that arrives today fails to have stories, if not entire sections, concerning our food: are we eating the right foods, too much food, too little of certain types, and on and on.

Especially in the sports world, one finds the unusual. For some readers, collecting stamps has a human interest approach. Humor can make an otherwise dull story interesting, as we'll see in the following examples.

Better Check Carefully

The *Sabetha Star* tells the following story: A woman and a boy get on a train with a full fare and a half fare ticket. "Madam, I can't take this ticket for the boy, he wears long pants," said the conductor. "All right," said the woman, "take the full ticket for him."

Cabool Enterprise, 3-27-1908

So Why Teach Sex?

On Saturday last morning about the time the sun had risen o'er the Illinois hills, a huge white bird with a very long bill, and carrying therewith a bundle weighing about eleven pounds, flew through the door at the residence of Mayor P. S. Terry and his wife, left the bundle which was addressed to the mayor and flew away. Upon examination the bundle was found to contain a fine baby boy weighing ten and a half pounds and Mayor Terry's fondest hopes and dreams had come true—a son who ere long will call him dad. The Mayor promptly proceeded to close his office and by proclamation, decreed that Saturday, July 5th, must henceforth be observed as a holiday. The *Tri-City Independent* extends congratulations to the happy parents and this move is heartily seconded by the City Council of Festus and attested by the City Clerk.

Festus Tri-City Independent, 7-11-1913

One of the Colonel's?

A South Missouri editor carries off the belt. He says: Some time ago our little baby's finger ring was missed and could not be found. When last seen the child had it on and was feeding some chickens, but no trace of it could be found, and the subject was dismissed until yesterday, when one of the hens came off with a brood of chickens, and, lo, behold around the neck of one of the tiny creatures was the baby's ring. Our presumption is that the hen swallowed the ring, but how on earth did it get around the little chicken's neck?

Huntsville Herald, 1-24-1894

Didn't You Know That?

Gumption is defined as the ability to put the grease where the squeak is found.

Ashland Bugle, 3-29-1906

A chasm that often separates friends: Sarcasm.

Unionville Investigator, 4-10-1886

True merit is like a river: the deeper it gets the less noise it makes.

Novinger Record, 5-18-1908

And More Useful Definitions

Politeness is like an air cushion—there may be nothing in it, but it eases our jobs wonderfully.

Kansas City Journal of Commerce, 1-13-1879

Fame is like a shaved pig with a greased tail, and it is only when it has slipped through the hands of some thousand, that some fellow by mere chance holds on to it.

Glasgow Times, 5-17-1849

Goodness is a contagious epidemic, and is spread only by good faith.

Ashland Bugle, 3-7-191

Size and Calories Studied

Small turkeys are better than big turkeys because there isn't so much hash on the small turkey.

Sikeston Standard, 12-13-1922

We know an old fellow who attended a catfish fry the other evening, took aboard a bottle of beer, one-fourth of a hot onion, a slab of fish as big as two hands, a mess of Irish potatoes, two cups of black coffee, and topped off with a cherry pie with whipped cream. Just why is it that a man's wife won't sympathize with him when he feels bad?

Sikeston Standard, 1-9-1948

Food: Nothing for Dessert?

Once upon a time a man thought he knew a mushroom from a toadstool. A large family survives him.

Salem Dent County Post, 10-3-1912

Classic Taste-Smell Test

To tell good eggs: Place the large end of the egg against the tongue, if it becomes immediately warm to the tongue, the egg is very fresh; if it becomes warm slowly, it is stale. If no heat is felt the egg is bad.

St. Louis Carondelet News, 4-4-1903

Eating onions not only prevents the lips from chapping, but usually keeps the chaps from lipping.

Clinton Advocate, 7-2-1885

The *Centralia Courier* says that it has come to its ears that, whereas an apple a day may keep the doctor away, an onion a day will keep everyone away.

Ashland Bugle, 2-9-1922

Stingy to the End

I know a very stingy man. When he died they put upon his monument this inscription: *continued*

"Here lies old 10 per cent; the more he made the less he spent;
the more he got the less he lent; he's dead, we don't know where
he went;
but if his soul to heaven is went, he'll own the place and charge
them rent."

Illmo Jumplicute, 1-4-1923

They say a man is very stingy when he will not enjoy a joke at his
own expense.

Rolla Standard, 4-22-1898

Sports Can Be Humorous

Some of the young men about Richmond were very much excited
last week when it was learned that the Grand Jury was investigating the
matter of their playing baseball on Sunday. We are not posted as to what
was done on the premises but if they were all heavily fined it would
serve them right. We haven't a particle of sympathy for a young man,
who has arrived at man's estate, who will deliberately go out upon a
vacant lot in the city, and with his associates, engage in a game, a part of
which consists in yelling at the top of his voice, on the Sabbath Day, to
the disturbance of quiet people in the neighborhood. It is bad enough on
the week day.

Richmond Democrat, 5-11-1882

No End to Golf

Promoted: Do you know what becomes of small boys who
used such bad language when they play marbles? George: Yes,
mum. They grow up and play golf.

EX *Poplar Bluff American Republic*, 1-2-1930

The social climber who has wasted his substance in golfing
outfits is now suffering from ping pongitis, a disease that is said to
be prevalent among American plutocrats.

Calhoun Clarion, 4-12-1902

A gentleman declares that a golfer can do no more than make a
hole in one—which is a perfect shot. Oh, yes he can. He can spend the
rest of his life telling about it.

Willow Springs News, 5-2-1935

And Turn Pro Early?

Should not the young men who sacrifice their education to the glory of their college on the football field, the diamond, and the water, receive pensions from their alma mater? There is a question for the trustees to discuss.

Chillicothe Constitution, 12-14-1890

Stamps Have a Place

A young man who spends his time loafing around stores and smoking cigarettes is just about as useful as a canceled postage stamp.

Carl Junction Graphic, 1-24-1907

Boys, if you would succeed like a postage stamp, stick to one thing until you get there.

Carl Junction Graphic, 2-16-1907

Women's Faces Stuck

The head of Martha Washington may adorn one of the new postage stamps. The first time woman ever got ahead on anything except talking.

Hardin News, 4-10-1902

A woman writer in the *Ladies' Home Journal* makes a plea for women's faces on the postage stamp instead of men's. If the mucilage was on that side it might do, but who would want to lick a woman's back?

Louisiana Press-Journal, 3-27-1902

Criminals Often Ahead

A new counterfeit fifty cent stamp is in circulation, which is said to be a decided improvement on the genuine.

Versailles Gazette, 5-27-1871

Sleep Has Its Place

Sleep is one of the blessings the busy man needs and the idle man does not know how to enjoy.

Hartsburg Truth, 10-11-1902

Hard luck is a polite name for a sleeping sickness.

Salem Post, 3-7-1918

In extra polite circles the nightmare is termed "the nocturnal horse of the feminine gender."

Palmyra Missouri Whig, 5-28-1846

Need a Better Definition?

Paddy's description of a fiddle cannot be beat: "It was the shape of a turkey, and the size of a goose; he turned it over on its back and rubbed the belly with a stick, and ouch! St. Patrick, how it did squeak!"

Fredericktown Conservative, 8-2-1862

Editors Often Focus on Themselves

One must never conclude that our pioneer editors occupied their time seeking topics that would focus primarily on the interests and concerns of their readers.

Editors loved to alert the public of their own difficulties, especially when their problems concerned financial status. Money was, of course, a primary topic. Readers too often—as least so the editors believed—borrowed a neighbor's copy rather than subscribe themselves.

And whenever a prominent individual offered kind words about the nation's newspapermen, the local editor was sure to reprint the account.

Unfortunately, some of today's readers are too young to realize that many of these newspapers were printed on slow presses, from copy written by hand on paper (not on computer stock). And the characters would be set in type one letter at a time; worst of all, these characters had to be returned to type cases for reuse.

But what history they have contributed to succeeding generations! Most editors sought the readers' sympathy. Some even deserved it.

Wonder What He Ate?

"The man who hunts up the cheapest printer is like the man who runs his finger down the prices of the bill of fare, and then looks to see what he gets for it."

Richmond News, 9-3-1914

Puns Then Too

About every paragrapher has taken a shot at the fact that a couple were married on a train in Pennsylvania the other day, but so far no one has mentioned it as being a "railroad tie."

Tarkio Atchison County World, 1-29-1903

Times Don't Change Either

Editing a newspaper is a pleasing business—if you can stand it.
If subscribers want to bawl out anybody the editor is the goat.
If the town is lagging behind and people won't get out and make things
    hum—it's because the town paper is on the bum.
If business is bad—it's because the editor wants too much money for his
    advertising space.
If business is good—advertising hasn't anything to do with it, but
    conditions are right.
If we print what pleases people—that is our duty and we deserve no
    credit.
If we print what is displeasing—we are a grouch and a crepe hanger, and
    don't deserve the patronage of the public.
If we print the news as it is actually—people call us over the phone and
    tell us to stop the paper.
If we garble it—they tell us we are subsidized by the corporate interest.
Editing a newspaper is a pleasing business—it is not!

Hartsburg Truth, 10-8-1915

An editor who can please everyone is not suited for this earth, but is entitled to wings. Human nature is so constituted that some of our readers would like to have us tell the unvarnished truth, while others assault us if we do.

Auxvasse Review, 6-1-1908

You've Been Warned

If there is any time that a man appreciates the newspaper's courtesy and kindness more than another it is when he gets in trouble and doesn't want the public to know about it. Verily, it behooves every man to be on friendly terms with the editor.

Aurora Advertiser, 11-17-1908

But More Interesting?

The Missouri editor who wrote the following items may have meant well but he was surely a shade careless on the way he scattered the English language around. The first item was "Mrs. Thomas Johnson read an article to the Women's Club entitled 'Personal

---

Devils.' Seventeen were present." The other: "Mr. John Crouse shipped a carload of hogs to Kansas City one day last week. Three of his neighbors went with him to help make up the load."

EX *Sikeston Standard*, 2-4-1919

Know Your Neighbors

Stranger: "And you say the editor died with his boots on?" Printer: "Yes, sir, you see he knew the town so well he wouldn't pull 'em off for fear they'd steal his socks."

Warrensburg Journal-Democrat, 1-1-1892

English Courses Might Help

The following note was sent to an Atchison county merchant: "Send me a trace-chain and two hinges. Jane had a baby last night—also two padlocks."

Sedalia Bazoo, 3-23-1873

A man stopping his paper, wrote the editor: "I think folks ottent to spend ther muny for payper mi dady diddent and everybody sed he was the intelligentest man in the country and had the smartest family of boiz that ever dugged taters."

Paris Monroe County Appeal, 4-11-1884

Lincoln Knew, Too

Newspaper readers like editorials that start quick and stop quicker.

Ashland Bugle, 1-9-1919

Must Have Priorities

A reporter in writing up a murder case said: "The murderer was evidently in search of money, but most fortunately the victim had lodged all his funds the day before in the bank, so after all he lost nothing but his life."

Carl Junction Graphic, 2-26-1907

◆

Some Such Men Around Today

A man remarked that he did not read the county papers. There is nothing in them. That same man did not know of a dozen events that had taken place in his town and which he was surprised to hear. He never read the editorials but every subject discussed in them was Greek to him. Yet he can vote.

Salem Republican, 2-21-1908

An Early Rush Limbaugh?

A California paper, alluding to a recent libel case, asks: "If a newspaper cannot call a man a bully and a blackguard and keep on doing so for a couple of weeks, where is the boasted liberty of the press?"

St. Louis Globe, 7-18-1872

Printers Have Problems

Walker, one of our compositors, says he knows water when he sees it, because it looks like gin.

Rock Port Democratic Mail, 9-5-1878

The labor of an editor's life is not so much what he has to write as what he has to read.

Fayette Boon's Lick Times, 2-3-1844

If you see a mistake in the *Sentinel* do not run to us with it. Only dead people make no mistakes. Besides, we saw it first.

Iberia Sentinel, 1-9-1914

Wonder Where It Went?

A Missouri editor is said to be slowly worrying himself to death over the question of what becomes of the wind when it doesn't blow.

Oak Grove Banner, 10-6-1905

The Absolute End

Jefferson City, MO. (AP) In the process of gathering old records together and photographing them for compact storage, Missouri's new Records Management Agency came up with some dandies. Secretary of State James C. Kirkpatrick, who oversees the Records Center, reported some of them Friday including these from old vital statistics records of death causes: "Went to bed feeling well but woke dead." "Died suddenly. Nothing serious." "Don't know. Died without the aid of a physician." "Blow on the head with an ax. Contributory cause, another man's wife." "Had never been fatally ill before."

St. Louis Globe-Democrat, 12-3-1966

Still a Needed Source

A newspaper but holds the mirror up to the nature and reflects the doings of the world good, bad, and indifferent. The mirror is not responsible for its face. Many a crime has been prevented through fear of newspaper publicity, and many a public and semi-public institution is run on correct lines through a wholesome dread of the newspapers.

Perry Enterprise, 1-11-1900

Ahead of the Computer

The lead pencil is noiseless, but a power in the land. We believe that newspaper men did not exist until the lead pencil was invented, and no editor could get along without his trusty soft lead smearer.

Montrose Tidings, 1-1-1919

And This in 1910?

A large number of newspapers having made such strenuous feature of the women's page leads a tired man subscriber to ask why somebody doesn't start a man's page. The world is getting so that a mere man doesn't count except when bill paying time arrives.

Joplin Times, 6-10-1910

Replace with Police?

The following remarks were made by evangelist Billy Sunday: "I believe that an honest newspaper is invincible. You can't stop it any more than you can sink a battleship with a shotgun, smash Gilbralter with a pea-shooter, or dam Niagara Falls with toothpicks and hair combs. If the newspapers were all suppressed, I believe that crime and sin would increase 100 per cent overnight and all hell would hold a jubilee."

Hartsburg Truth, 9-3-1915

The Truth CAN Hurt

A Missouri woman is suing an editor because he said in an obituary that her husband had gone to a happier home. All editors should know by this time that it never pays to say what you think.

EX *Hartsburg Truth*, 7-5-1907

Needed in Washington

We read a piece the other day about three stingy men. One of them would not drink as much water as wanted, unless it was from another man's well. The second forbid any of his family from writing anything except in small hand as it is a waste of ink to make large letters. The third stops his clock at night in order to save the wear and tear of the machinery. All of them decline to take their home paper on the ground that it is a terrible strain on their spectacles to read newspapers, even in day time.

Hartsburg Truth, 12-20-1907

Still the Same

Some people can never understand the fact that a newspaper is not responsible for the opinions and utterances of its contributors. The newspaper is the people's forum and the contributor who speaks through its columns does not in any way reflect the opinions, or the sentiments of the publisher.

Aurora Advertiser, 3-27-1908

You've Been Warned

An irate female seeks admittance to the editor's sanctum. "But, I tell you, madam," protests the attendant, "that the editor is too ill to talk to anyone today." "Never mind, you let me in. I'll do the talking."

Sedalia Central Missouri Sentinel, 12-18-1886

But More Interesting?

Definition of News: This is the way an exchange asks for news: "If you know of anything we don't know which people ought to know, if it is worth knowing don't you know it is your duty to let us know that the people may also know that you know that you know what we ought to know, but don't know because you know, but won't let us know."

EX *Maysville DeKalb County Herald,* April 1934.

An Editor Should Know

An editor acknowledges the receipt of brandy forty-eight years old, and said: "This brandy is so old we fear it cannot live much longer."

Paris Mercury, 4-22-1873

Course in English Might Help

When you see italics in print it is a sign the writer is using words of which he doesn't comprehend the meaning.

Lexington Intelligencer, 5-2-1891

Better Be Quiet

The man who gets mad at what the newspapers say about him, should return thanks three times a day for what the newspapers know about him but don't print.

Fulton Sun, 10-27-1893

Politically Correctness?

We notice in an exchange that the house of a widow woman in Montgomery City was burglarized the other night. Perhaps if she had been a widow man this wouldn't have happened.

Louisiana Press-Journal, 3-27-1902

Same Problem Today?

The daily press of today is to blame for much of the crime. They make a specialty of murder, hold-ups, suicides and disgraceful love affairs, and one crime leads to another. Many people are so constituted that they will take the risk of hanging to get their picture and stories of their affairs in the daily paper. It goes in waves and the more of such sensational matter the papers publish the more cases there are of the same stripe. With the paper muzzled from publishing such news for six months it is certain crime would grow less.

Edina Democrat, 3-9-1906

Yes, the *Standard* is just a little different from the average county weekly. We most generally give the news, then throw in a few views without extra cost, carry a few paragraphs to amuse and a few that sometimes annoy. Anyway, read every page as you might find what you are looking for, but don't want to see in print.

Sikeston Standard, 2-13-1931

We believe every newspaper ought to speak its honest sentiments on every question that confronts it. Some times it appears to be bad policy to do so, but it will find itself respected the more for it in the long run.

Paris Monroe County Appeal, 11-27-1885

The Press Reports on Crime

A judge in North Missouri has decided that it is criminal negligence to get close to the heels of a mule.

Rolla Times, 5-19-1910

Traveling in Good Company

"The rural press, the pulpit and the school are a trinity of powerful influences that the farmer must utilize to their fullest capacity before he can occupy a commanding position in public affairs," said Peter Radford, lecturer, National Farmer Union. He added: "It is the local press that will study the local problems and through its columns deal with subjects of most vital importance to local life in the community."

Hartsburg Truth, 3-26-1915

Better Pay for Subscription

A man who won't take a paper because he can borrow one, has invented a machine with which he can cook his dinner by the smoke of his neighbor's chimney.

Huntsville North Missouri Herald, 2-10-1869

Now is the accepted time to propose to the editor—propose that he give you the paper for a year for a dollar and he will accept.

Holden Progress, 12-31-1904

A Linn county editor intends to be present with a carefully prepared list at the "old settlers" reunion at Linneus September 12 just to remind a few of the old settlers that they haven't settled.

Monett Eagle, 9-4-1903

Sound Familiar?

A statistician has figured that sixty-seven murders out of every one hundred may be traced directly to the "pistol toting" habit. The proposition to force "pistol toters" to wear badges may have a fine and effective point after all.

Graham Post, 2-4-1909

The next thing to the person "who didn't know it was loaded" is the one who puts a stick of dynamite in the stove to thaw it out.

Platte City Landmark, 2-23-1894

No Alimony Either?

"A Chicago man has been sent to the penitentiary for marrying fifty women," says the *Johnson Democrat*. It is sometimes necessary to adopt heroic measures to protect men from themselves.

Graham Post, 3-4-1909

Women are attaining that equality with a vengeance in the eyes of the courts, an Ohio judge has compelled a woman to pay alimony.

Cole Camp Courier, 10-24-1901

What, No Parole?

An anti-chicken thief society has been organized at Clarence, Shelby County, and the next offender caught will be harshly treated. Three methods of punishment are under discussion—hanging, a coat of tar and feathers and the whipping post.

Cedar City Chronicle, 8-16-1900

Better Buy Your Own

Bob Smith, a Fulton negro, broke an ax handle over his wife's head the other day and she had him arrested for destroying private property. The handle belonged to Mrs. Smith.

Hartsburg Truth, 7-17-1903

Other Wit and Wisdom
Too Good to Pass Up

In a review of more than two thousand of these pithy sayings, there are many that appear to cross categories or fail to find their proper niche. Many quips cover several topics and have the quality to provide for editorial comments even today.

They are included here, since many could be used in educational circles, at home or in schools. Others could inspire ministers while they seek for appropriate topics for upcoming sermons. And, too, they help the writer here in collecting everything that's left over.

Where there are several related items, they have been grouped, such as this first unit concerning accidents. Other areas follow.

Some Celebration

Willie lit some powder sticks,
Willie's funeral July six.

Ashland Bugle, 6-30-1938

Hot Panties

Some seem to think that the fire at the Cut-Rate Mercantile House on New Madrid Street Sunday morning was caused by spontaneous combustion that started in the front window that was filled with women's panties.

Sikeston Standard, 1-9-1948

What a Fire!

The village of Sweet Home, in Nodaway county, was almost totally destroyed by fire recently. Only one house was left standing. Before the fire there were two.

Troy Lincoln County Herald, 2-10-1870

Careful with Your Time

The way to acquire leisure is to make the best of your time.

Aurora Advertiser, 11-12-1909

Hint to Teachers

It's better to bring the bottom up to the top than to pull the top down to the bottom.

Ashland Bugle, 11-22-1917

Life IS What You Make It

Any man who thinks he has no chance is correct.

Jefferson City Capital News, 1-24-1922

Impudence and audacity will often accomplish more than modesty and wisdom, but their victories are short lived.

Lathrop Monitor-Herald, 1-31-1907

It is with faded beauty as with a clock—the more the face is enameled the more clearly do we see the progress of time.

Oregon Holt County News, 7-17-1857

Just Can't Win Them All

Whatever you do, remember there's somebody it won't suit. The only people who have no enemies are those who do nothing and instead of hate they get contempt.

Lamar Democrat, 4-8-1908

Readers, did you ever notice that the man you done most for, was the first to turn on you when in a tight place?

Palmyra Missouri Whig, 11-13-1851

To Lead or Not to Lead?

When you have an ax to grind use your own grindstone.

Lexington Caucasion, 1-13-1894

The desire to have other people live according to our ideas seems to be inherent in many of us.

Marshall Democrat News, 1-13-1916

Don'ts for the Day

Do not ask for a better day,
Ask that you may live it a better way.

Ashland Bugle, 11-14-1940

A don't for the day: Don't think a man is a fool because he looks funny. Likewise, don't take it for granted that he is not a fool if he doesn't look funny.

Sikeston Standard, 3-13-1914

When a pocketbook or a mouth is opened too often nothing is left in it.

Ashland Bugle, 3-3-1921

The man who refuses to take advice is the freest to give it unasked.

Richmond Missourian, 9-5-1901

Road Signs for Life

A head never swells to make room for brains.

Sturgeon Leader, 11-14-1901

It's hard to throw mud without besmearing yourself.

Urich Herald, 6-8-1911

You and That Tree

Looking an oak tree square in the eye, there's nothing that should discourage you. It was once a nut, too.

Ashland Bugle, 9-3-1924

This Is Toleration?

Some people's idea of toleration: "Do as I want you to do, and think as I want you to think, and you will be liberal."

Rock Port Sun, 1-19-1882

How's Your Bank Account?

You don't need references in order to borrow trouble.

Flat River Lead Belt News, 12-17-1915

Death Has Its Day

The undertaker usually finishes all he undertakes.

Neosho Miner and Mechanic, 9-16-1910

Death has consigned many a man of fame whom longer life would have consigned to infamy.

Richfield Enterprise, 12-16-1854

Women's Age a Mystery

A woman gets so old that she no longer cares to marry. But usually a man never does.

Lamar Democrat, 5-6-1909

This is woman's age, but on this point at least she is silent.

Ashland Bugle, 11-3-1921

Years that should be serene
Often are the ones that are lean.

Ashland Bugle, 2-8-1939

Compare the Animals

It's a pity that some animals can't talk and some men can.

Cuba Review, 3-14-1918

On April Fool Day

April Fool's Day has come and gone and we suppose there are just as many now as there was before.

Sikeston Standard, 4-3-1914

Glorious news is soon expected from Jefferson (City). There are hopes that the Legislature will adjourn April 1st—a most fitting day for such a deed.

Carrollton Wakanda Record, 3-15-1872

Automobiles Seldom Change

It's easy to hitch your wagon to a star, but parking your auto is a different proposition.

Ashland Bugle, 6-6-1918

Between wives and automobiles some men have difficulty in telling which is the greater luxury.

Montrose Tidings, 1-2-1919

More than a million new telephone poles were erected last year, and several million automobiles were built to climb them.

Puxico Herald, 4-10-1930

Covered by Medicare?

A bachelor physician declares the microbes in kisses are often fatal—at least they often develop matrimonial germs.

Graham Post, 4-8-1909

A bachelor says that love is a combination of diseases—an affection of the heart and an inflammation of the brain.

Cole Camp Courier, 11-21-1901

No Better Excuse

The president of a bachelor's club at Nevada, Mo., has resigned to get married. The presumption is that he grew tired of being at the head of things.

Jonesburg Journal, 2-1-1906

Who Gets Last Laugh?

An old bachelor who bears his lonely state with such equanimity says, "It is better to be laughed at for not being married than to be unable to laugh because you are."

Paris Mercury, 4-1-1873

Bored—A Two-Way Street

When you are bored console yourself. You will have a chance probably to bore some one else before the day is over.

Stoutsville Banner, 1-25-1900

A bore is a person given to talking about himself to you at the moment you wish to talk about yourself to him.

Willow Springs News, 8-1-1935

Can We Do Without Fools?

If it were not for the fools, the way of the wise would be all uphill.

Lockwood Luminary, 2-21-1913

The money and hair of a fool are soon parted in the middle.

Savannah Reporter, 5-12-1876

An industrious fool can keep three or four wise people at work repairing damages.

Stockton Cedar County Republican, 1-24-1890

It's easy for a man to make a fool of himself—in fact, most fools are self-made.

Huntsville Randolph Democrat, 1-19-1900

Could Collect in Washington

In old days they spoke of a licensed fool. If all the fools were required to have a license now the government could do away with its other taxes and still maintain the surplus. There's a "single tax" for you.

Hartsburg Truth, 10-4-1902

Watch What They Say

It is well to take warning from the silly as counsel from the wise.

Weston Chronicle, 2-7-1896

Don't think because you can fool some people that others can't fool you.
West Plains Journal, 12-22-1898

Many a man will merely smile if you call him a scoundrel. But just call him a fool and he's hopping mad.
Lamar Democrat, 3-18-1909

The foolish man can ask twice as many questions as the wise can answer.
Graham Post, 3-18-1909

A man who doesn't know anything will tell it the first time he gets a chance.
Ste. Genevieve Fair Play, 8-1-1872

Humor Helps Us to Survive

"Just fancy that!" exclaimed the proud mother. "They've promoted our Herbert for hitting a sergeant! They've made him a court martial."
Memphis Democrat, 6-4-1942

Mrs. Gleeson (at concert): "She has quite a large repertoire, hasn't she?" Gleeson: "Yes, and that dress makes it look all the worse."
Kahoka Gazette-Herald, 4-5-1935

There is more benefit in a good laugh than in all the hot water remedies—cold water, electric and all the other new fangled treatments in the world and it does not cost anything. Laugh. If you have nothing else to laugh at, laugh at your neighbor. He is probably improving his health by laughing at you.
Essex Leader, 4-4-1913

How to Escape Trouble

You can easily keep yourself throughout the winter from freezing, by getting continually into hot water with your neighbor.
Oregon Holt County Sentinel, 6-30-1865

A little humor often lifts one over a dark and difficult place. It takes the sting out of worries and shows the folly of borrowing trouble.

Sikeston Standard, 5-29-1914

And What of the Third Trip?

"Pop, a man's wife is his better half, isn't she?" "So we are told, my son." "Then if a man married twice there isn't anything left of him, is there?"

Gainesville Ozark County Times, 10-4-1907

Price Tag for Husband

A woman went into a newspaper office and wished to advertise for her husband who had disappeared. When told they charged two dollars an inch, she went out, saying it would break her up at that rate as her husband was over six feet tall.

Auxvasse Review, 11-25-1909

To Be or Not To Be

I regard a sense of humor as one of the most precious gifts that can be vouch-safed to a human being. He is not necessarily a better man for having it, but he is a happier one. It renders him to enjoy his own discomfiture. Blessed with this sense he is never unduly elated or cast down. No one can ruffle his temper. No abuse disturbs his equanimity. Bores do not bore him. Humbugs do not humbug him. Solemn airs do not impose on him. Titles and decorations are but childish baubles in his eyes. Prejudice does not warp his judgment. He is never in conceit or out of conceit himself. He abhors all dogmatism. The world is a stage on which actors strut and fret for his edification and amusement, and he pursues the even current of his way, invulnerable, doing what is right and proper according to his lights, but utterly indifferent, whether he does find approval or disapproval from others. If Hamlet had any sense of humor he would not have been a nuisance to himself and to all surrounding him.

Columbia Missouri Herald, 12-16-1898

Laughter Has Its Value

Laugh first, laugh last and laugh all the time during a political campaign.

Ashland Bugle, 4-15-1904

A laugh is worth a hundred groans in any market.

Hartsburg Truth, 4-5-1907

Laughing is the best medicine, but not when you are being laughed at.

Ashland Bugle, 5-19-1904

You can't live forever and you won't even live half that long if you don't cheer up.

Lewistown Record, 7-15-1920

Lying Creates Problems

Lying is the most unprofitable vice, and pretention to knowledge not possessed is a common form of lying.

Hartsburg Truth, 11-1-1902

There must be some good use for liars in the world, or there wouldn't be so many of them.

Salem News, 2-22-1923

If an untruth is only a day old it is called a lie; if it is a year old it is called a falsehood; but if it is a century old it is called a legend.

Kansas City Star, 10-16-1990

Obviously a Clear Scene

The naked truth about humanity isn't very difficult to discuss in these modern times.

Lancaster Excelsior, 2-1-1923

The worst feature about a pretty view or sunset is that the sight seems to make too many people imagine they can write poetry.

Mt. Vernon Lawrence Chieftain, 1-6-1898

Patience, Just Patience

A Quaker Woman's Sermon—Dear Friends: There are three things I very much wonder at. The first is, that children should be so foolish as to throw up stones, clubs and brickbats into fruit trees, to knock down the fruit; if they would let it alone it would fall. The second is, that men should be so foolish and even so wicked as to get into war and kill each other; if left alone they would die themselves. And the third and last thing that I wonder at is that young men should be so unwise as to go after young women; if they would stay at home, the young women would go after them.

Memphis Reveille, 1-6-1866

Who Threw the Hammer?

THAT HAMMER—Yesterday afternoon a man who was seen running down stairs from one of our upstairs saloons, just before him was a hammer and in advance of the hammer another man was flying into the street. The hammer missed the man and struck a boy, who gave a yell and darted against a Dutch woman, who was carrying a basket of eggs in one hand and a jug of molasses in the other, knocked her down and she landed upon his eggs, while the jug flew from her hand and, striking the pavement, spread its content over the walk. A man running along with his hands in his pockets, stepped into the molasses and his feet flying from under him, he fell on the woman, who gave a yell which frightened a team of horses that were standing near, and they broke loose and ran up the street, demolished the wagon and scattering the contents on the payment. The question is who threw the hammer, and is he responsible for the subsequent chapter of accidents?

Oregon Holt County Sentinel, 4-27-1866

Poetry Can Tell Story

We know a Sturgeon boy so lazy, 'Tis a wonder that he grows,
He sits around and waits, For the wind to blow his nose.

Sturgeon Leader, 12-5-1901

Smile awhile—While you smile—Another smiles—And soon there's miles and miles of smiles—And life's worthwhile—If you but smile.

Cabool Enterprise, 8-17-1906

Smith had a lovely baby girl, the Stork left her with a flutter. Smith named her Oleomargarine, for he hadn't any but her.

Auxvasse Review, 5-4-1911

"A Missouri poet," observes the *Louisiana Times,* "has written a poem knocking on the incubator. He is right. It always seemed wrong to beat an old hen out of a job with a tin box and coal oil lamp."

Vienna Maries County Gazette, 4-17-1914

Professors and Press Collide

Another "professor" has come to the front. He has discovered that it is possible to hypnotize a grasshopper. What would the country do without her "professors"?

Jasper News, 9-12-1901

A Chicago professor says there are more insane persons in this country than college students. Some professors possibly?

Lockwood Luminary, 3-7-1913

Queer things are these college professors. The latest freak idea advanced by one of them is that all children are natural born liars. Children are not all liars any more than college professors are all fools.

Aurora Advertiser, 2-5-1909

Time Fits Narrow Role

Time is never lost that is spent in leading any person into a better life.

Hartsburg Truth, 10-11-1907

Better three hours too soon than one minute too late.

Owensville Gasconade County Republican, 2-28-1903

A punctual man is very rarely a poor man.

Richfield Monitor, 12-8-1855

People seldom realize what a good time they are having until it is over.

Sedalia Daily Capital, 1-6-1911

Don't waste other people's time while you are wasting your own.

Rockville Booster, 8-21-1908

Even an Umbrella Humorous

It frequently rains on the just because the unjust has carried off his umbrella.

Skidmore Standard, 9-23-1898

What an awful amount of umbrella buying and stealing there must have been during the early days of the deluge.

Washington Franklin County Democrat, 1-2-1880

A newly married man has discovered the difference between an umbrella and a woman is that you can sometimes shut up the umbrella.

Kansas City Star, 10-7-1880

If Nothing Else, the Weather

The editor of an exchange got excited when talking about this dry weather and said he visited a section of the country where there were "Bull frogs three years old that couldn't swim."

Urich Herald, 8-10-1911

James Miller of Fulton recalls that 1854 was a terribly dry year. "It was during the roasting ear season of this year," says he, "that my father ate at one meal fourteen acres of corn."

Blackburn Record, 8-2-1901

And It Only Gets Worse

The "worst yet" story of the drouth comes from Lexington, says an exchange, where a farmer is said to have been feeding his hens cracked ice to prevent them from laying hard-boiled eggs.

Cole Camp Courier, 8-15-1901

A Kansas paper says that during the past drouth, the water in the streams of that state was so low that frogs jumped in backward to keep from skinning their noses.

Jameson Gem, 10-2-1913

Weather Always Unusual?

When the weather bureau predicts rain three days in succession and it fails to materialize, it turns about and predicts clear weather. That brings it.

Excelsior Springs Call, 5-10-1906

Missouri weather has become as uncertain as Missouri politics.

Lawson Ray County Review, 2-18-1909

The weather is one of the things that can please but a few people at a time.

Hume Border Telephone, 9-5-1896

Now That Is Cold!

Winter of 1855-56. On the night of the 24th of December, 1855, the Missouri River at this place was frozen over. It is now near five weeks that the river has been a highway for teams of horses, mules, and oxen. We put this fact on record for coming years. A season unparalleled in the history of this country. People will hereafter refer to the "long winter of 1855-56."

(The newspaper reported on March 1, 1856, that "The river at this place broke up on Monday morning last, the 25th of February, having been closed sixty-one days.")

Kansas City Enterprise, 1-26-1856

And In Conclusion!

Youth and age have too little sympathy for each other. If the young would remember that they may be old, and the old remember that they were once young the world would be happier.

Paris Monroe County Appeal, 2-4-1881

Indian or Brave?

Indian braves used to sit around in a circle and pass the pipe. White braves sit around in a circle and pass the bottle and the buck.

Kansas City Times, 11-19-1935

Last Word on Politics

It's truth that shall make you free, not politics. Politics is generally free from truth.

Ashland Bugle, 7-4-1919

Have faith in your country, your business, your fellow man. Nobody ever played the United States short and won.

Sikeston Standard, 1-18-1921

The difference between a hen and a candidate for president is that the hen cackles after she's laid the egg, the presidential candidate before.

Ashland Bugle, 4-22-1920

Longevity is a good thing, only public men overdo it. To die at the proper time and leave a good impression on history seems to be one of the lost arts.

Ashland Bugle, 9-25-1919

About the Author

For more than 35 years, Dr. William H. Taft taught journalism, the last 25 years at the University of Missouri-Columbia. His special research concerned Missouri newspapers, and he has written three books on this topic.

In this latest volume, Dr. Taft reveals the lighter side of the editors' duties, showing how knowledgeable they were on diverse subjects, together with their willingness to write as they felt, regardless of the outcome.

Dr. Taft, born in Mexico, Mo., graduated from Westminster College, University of Missouri and the Western Reserve University. Retired in 1981 as Professor Emeritus from the University of Missouri-Columbia Journalism School, he continues as historian of the Missouri Press Association and remains involved in other research projects.

Previous books by Taft include *Missouri Newspapers* (University of Missouri Press, 1964); *Missouri Newspapers: When and Where, 1808-1963,* a listing of more than 6,000 newspapers that have appeared in the state (State Historical Society of Missouri, 1964); *Newspapers as Tools for Historians* (Lucas Brothers, 1967); *American Magazines for the 1980s* (Hastings House, New York, 1982); *Encyclopedia of Twentieth-Century Journalists* (Garland, New York, 1986); *Missouri Newspapers and the Missouri Press Association: 125 Years of Service, 1867-1992* (Heritage House, 1992). He has also published numerous encyclopedia articles, *Journalism Quarterly* articles and others.

He began his newspaper career as a teenager on the *Mexico Ledger*, writing "locals" and a high school column. At Westminster he handled public relations. He has taught at Youngston, Hiram and Defiance Colleges in Ohio, and founded the journalism program at Memphis State University prior to returning to Columbia in 1956. He has been married for more than 55 years to his wife, Myrtle, and they have three children.

Index

NOTE: Starting and ending dates of Missouri newspapers remain a confused topic with many publications. Data above from Taft, *Missouri Newspapers: When and Where 1808-1963* and from updated research completed by the State Historical Society of Missouri. Often newspapers went through name changes, further confusing the problem.

The Show Me Missouri Series

99 Fun Things To Do
ISBN: 0-9646625-2-3
in Columbia & Boone County
Guide to 99 hidden highlights, unique dining, galleries, museums, towns, people and history in Columbia, Rocheport, Centralia and Boone County. Most trips are free or under $10. Includes maps, photos, accessibility of sites. Fully indexed. 168 pages. By Pamela Watson. $12.95

A to Z Missouri
ISBN: 0-9646625-4-X

Abo to Zwanzig! A dictionary-style book of Missouri place name origins. Includes history for each town and community, pronunciations, population, county, post office dates and more. 220 pages. By Margot Ford McMillen. $14.95

Best of Missouri Hands
ISBN: 0-9646625-5-8

Profiles of Missouri's fine artists and craftsmen. From porcelain to wood and pewter to gold, *Best of Missouri Hands* shows the best our state has to offer. This book highlights many traditional art forms and techniques, and the artists behind the expressions. 152 pages. By Brett Dufur. $12.95

Exploring Missouri Wine Country
ISBN: 0-9646625-6-6

This guidebook to Missouri Wine Country offers an intimate look at Missouri's winemakers and wineries, including how to get there, their histories and the story of how Missouri came to have its own Rhineland. Includes wine tips, recipes, home-brew recipes, dictionary of wine terms and more. Also lists nearby Bed and Breakfasts and lodging. 168 pages. By Brett Dufur. $14.95

Famous Missourians Who Made History
ISBN: 0-9646625-9-0

A book of easily digestible history, for school children and adults alike, of short stories and humorous comic-style illustrations of more than 50 Missourians who made a contribution to the state or nation. Compiled by Brett Dufur. $14.95

Forgotten Missourians Who Made History
ISBN: 0-9646625-8-2

A book of short stories and humorous comic-style illustrations of more than 50 Missourians who made a contribution to the state or nation yet are largely forgotten by subesquent generations. Companion book to *Famous Missourians Who Made History*. Compiled by Jim Borwick and Brett Dufur. $14.95

The Complete Katy Trail Guidebook

ISBN: 0-9646625-0-7

The most complete guide to services, towns, people, places and history along Missouri's 200-mile Katy Trail. This updated edition covers the cross-state hiking and biking trail from Clinton to St. Charles — now America's longest rails-to-trails project. Includes trailhead maps, 80 photos, Flood of '93, how to make blueberry wine, uses for Missouri mud and more. 168 pages. By Brett Dufur. $14.95

What's That?

ISBN: 0-9646625-1-5

A Nature Guide to the Missouri River Valley

Companion guide to the *Katy Trail Guidebook*. This easy-to-use, illustrated four-season guide identifies trees, flowers, birds, animals, insects, rocks, fossils, clouds, reptiles, footprints and more. Features the Missouri River Valley's most outstanding sites and nature daytrips. 176 pages. Compiled by Brett Dufur. $14.95

Wit & Wisdom

ISBN: 0-9646625-3-1

of Missouri's Country Editors

A compilation of over 600 pithy sayings from pioneer Missouri newspapers. Many of these quotes and quips date to the 19th century yet remain timely for today's readers. Richly illustrated and fully indexed to help you find that perfect quote. 168 pages. By William Taft. $14.95

Pebble Publishing

P.O. Box 431 ❖ Columbia, MO 65205-0431

(800) 576-7322 ❖ Fax: (573) 698-3108

Quantity	Book Title	x Unit Price =	Total

Mo. residents add 6.975% sales tax = ------------

Shipping ($1.24 each book) x = ------------

Total = ------------

Name:_____

Address:_____ Apt._____

City, State, Zip_____

Phone: (_____) _____

Credit Card # _____

Expiration Date _____/_____/_____   Please send catalog _____

Visit *Trailside Books* online at http://www.trailsidebooks.com

S how Me Missouri books are available at many local bookstores. They can also be ordered directly from the publisher, using this form, or ordered by phone, fax or over the Internet.

Pebble Publishing also distributes 100 other books of regional interest, rails-to-trails, Missouri history, heritage, nature, recreation and more. These are available through our online bookstore and mail-order catalog. Visit our online bookstore, called *Trailside Books* at http://www.trailsidebooks.com, or leave a message at brett@trailsidebooks.com. If you would like to receive our catalog, please fill out and mail the form on the previous page.